The Daniel Fast

The Daniel Fast

Biblical and Scientific Facts

Muzi Maseko

WIPF & STOCK · Eugene, Oregon

THE DANIEL FAST
Biblical and Scientific Facts

Copyright © 2017 Muzi Maseko. All rights reserved. Except for brief quotations in critical publications or reviews, no part of this book may be reproduced in any manner without prior written permission from the publisher. Write: Permissions, Wipf and Stock Publishers, 199 W. 8th Ave., Suite 3, Eugene, OR 97401.

Wipf & Stock
An Imprint of Wipf and Stock Publishers
199 W. 8th Ave., Suite 3
Eugene, OR 97401

www.wipfandstock.com

PAPERBACK ISBN: 978-1-5326-3150-4
HARDCOVER ISBN: 978-1-5326-3152-8
EBOOK ISBN: 978-1-5326-3151-1

Manufactured in the U.S.A.   OCTOBER 6, 2017

This book is dedicated to my wife Mokgadi,
who is my best friend, partner in ministry, and fellow
researcher in cardiovascular pathophysiology.
A special mention to my three children,
Thembi, Zintle, and Sibusiso, who are my inspiration.

Contents

Preface | ix

Chapter 1   Historical Background of the Daniel Fast | 1
Chapter 2   Eating Is the Original Sin | 7
Chapter 3   What to Do During the Fast | 13
Chapter 4   Knowing God | 33
Chapter 5   Why Don't We Eat Meat during the Daniel Fast? | 41
Chapter 6   Hunger Is the Best Cure | 49
Chapter 7   Fruits and Vegetables Are God's Medicines | 55
Chapter 8   The Daniel Fast for People who Are Overweight or Obese | 73
Chapter 9   The Daniel Fast for People with Diabetes | 79
Chapter 10   The Daniel Fast for People with Hypertension | 87
Chapter 11   The Daniel Fast for Teenagers | 93
Chapter 12   The Daniel Fast for the Elderly | 99

Conclusion | 105

Preface

Throughout recorded history, mankind has been plagued by numerous diseases that have caused the death and incapacitation of millions. This is in direct contrast to the perfect God who created all things. We know him as a loving and caring Father, yet there is so much suffering and death in his creation. Why does the nature of creation contradict the nature of the Creator? When we study the scriptures, it becomes clear that it was not like that in the beginning. There is a point in history where there was a transition from order to chaos. In the beginning, all of God's creation was in perfect harmony. There was neither sin nor sickness. Man and nature were in perfect harmony under the watchful eye of an omnipotent God.

It all began to fall apart in the third chapter of Genesis when man sinned against God. Mankind's sin contaminated the whole of creation. The whole universe moved from a state of order to disorder. Decay, sickness, diseases, and death entered the universe. This represents a scientific phenomenon called "enthalpy," also known as the Second Law of Thermodynamics. In simple terms, this law states that things tend to move from order to disorder. Spontaneous processes lead to an increase in the entropy of the universe. For example, heating diamonds produces hot carbon dioxide, but hot carbon dioxide does not spontaneously contract

ix

to form diamonds. Why does the universe tend to move towards disorder? Is this just a spontaneous process? This will be discussed in detail in chapter 2. We live in a fallen world. There are forces of darkness that propagate processes and events towards disorder, chaos and decay. Paul explains this phenomenon clearly in the book of Romans: "For creation was subjected to frustration, not by its own choice, but by the will of the one who subjected it, in hope that the creation itself will be liberated from its bondage to decay and brought into the glorious freedom of the children of God" (Rom 8:20–21).[1] This law of decay exerts its effects from tiny sub-atomic particles to mega gas giants in space. Human beings are not exempt from the effects of this force. From the moment a baby takes its first breath, the law of decay starts ravaging its tiny body. Paul states this very well: "So we do not lose heart. Though our outer self is wasting away, our inner self is being renewed day by day." (2 Cor 4:16). From the moment we are born, the law of disorder starts exerting its effects and our outer self; i.e., our bodies start wasting away. We thank God that we are not defenseless against these forces. Through fasting, God has given us the ability to control the rate at which our bodies degenerate. This concept of decay will be discussed in detail in chapter 11 when we deliberate on the age paradox.

The advent of medical science brought a glimmer of hope. With this technological advancement most diseases, especially infections, were brought under control. Major breakthroughs in medical science came with the discovery of antibiotics in 1928 by the Scottish biologist Sir Alexander Fleming. This discovery had a profound impact on history, because we saw a decrease in infant mortality and a general increase in lifespan of the human population. Mankind seemed to have gained an upper hand. However, as these infectious diseases were on a decline, a new threat surfaced; diseases of lifestyle took center stage. This epidemiological transition from infectious diseases to diseases of lifestyle is a well-known worldwide phenomenon. It's a transition that follows

---

1. I used two main translations in almost equal proportions; the English Standard Version (ESV) and the New International Version (NIV).

Preface

industrialization and migration of people from rural farming areas to cities. City life is characterized by the convenience of fast foods and processed foods, which lead to development of diseases of lifestyle like hypertension, type-2 diabetes, coronary artery diseases, cancer, and kidney problems. In spite of advances in medical science, these diseases are still the major causes of morbidity and mortality in the developing and developed world. This problem is compounded by the resurfacing of infectious diseases that had been eradicated by antibiotics. New strains of antibiotic-resistant bacteria "superbugs" have emerged. More people are dying from infectious diseases. Clearly, medical science has no lasting solutions. What about diseases of genetic origin? Are we winning that battle? Currently most of those diseases cannot be cured, but only controlled. Scientists are currently working on genotype-specific treatment for these conditions using a new technique called "gene therapy," a new field of medicine with a lot of potential. Through genetic diagnosis, individuals at risk of particular diseases will be diagnosed and given treatment specific for their genotype. Medical scientists are very excited about this new field of medicine, due to its potential to wipe out most diseases. Whether this will work or not is questionable. Based on the current evidence, it is unlikely to work because like the previous attempts, it is merely addressing the symptoms and not the root problem. The problem is beyond the realm of science—it is a spiritual problem. It began in the Garden of Eden when man sinned against God.

When Adam sinned against God, his sin contaminated all of creation. He unleashed a force that assimilated the whole of creation to the molecular level across all space-time. Though the effects of this force manifest physically in things like chaos, disorder, diseases, death, and decay, it is a spiritual force. All the chaos in the world, from sicknesses to natural disasters, has a spiritual origin. It is a spiritual and not a scientific approach that will bring a permanent solution. Only God's saving grace can give us a lasting solution. Sadly, in this postmodern world, the major philosophical system is epistemological pluralism that rejects any form of authority. The Christian hierarchal structure that sets God above all else does not suit the postmodern lifestyle. Biblical statements like, "You shall have no other gods before me" (Exod 20:3) or "I am the way and the truth and the life, no one comes to the Father except through me" (John 14:6) are seen as offensive. That is why Christians must fast and walk close with God if they don't want to be lost in the post-modern vortex of confusion.

INTRODUCTION

An apple a day keeps the doctor away. This is not just an idiomatic expression but a scientific fact. Research has shown that the more fruit and vegetables you eat, the healthier you become and the longer you live. A study conducted to assess the health benefits of consuming fruits and vegetables revealed that individuals who had three servings of fruits and vegetables a day reduced their chance of suffering a stroke by 11 percent, and those who had a serving of five fruits and vegetables a day reduced their chance of suffering a stroke by 21 percent. There was a clear negative linear relationship between a stroke and the consumption of fruits and vegetables, indicating that the more fruit and vegetable an individual consumes, the less likely they are to suffer a stroke. A number of study surveys reveal that adults who consume more fruits and vegetables have a lower risk of death than those who eat less. It is generally accepted that taking five portions of fruits and vegetables a day is sufficient, but recent research has shown that up to seven portions a day are required. In some countries this recommendation has been made standard, but in other countries they are still struggling to eat just five portions a day. In South Africa, the situation is much worse. In a study I conducted in 1996, I was able to show that potassium intake is far below the recommended daily allowance. Since fruits and vegetables are the source of potassium, the low levels indicate reduced fruit and vegetable consumption. In a related study I conducted in 2014, I was able to show that people who consume foods with high potassium content have a lower blood pressure compared to people with low potassium intake. Since high blood pressure leads to strokes, heart attacks, and

Preface

kidney failure, it is clear why a diet with a high proportion of fruits and vegetables is beneficial.

The Daniel Fast is a fruit- and vegetable-based fast that is inspired by the story of Daniel in chapters 1 and 10 of the book of Daniel in the Bible. In chapter 1, Daniel and his friends choose to eat only vegetables, rather than the palace food that was provided. After ten days, he and his friends are found to be healthier than the other captives who ate the palace food. In chapter 10, Daniel decides to fast for twenty-one days, and during that period he abstains from meat and choice foods. On the twenty-first day, he gets a spiritual breakthrough when an angel brings him an answer from God. Inspired by this story, modern-day Christians have adopted this type of fasting. It is popularly known as the Daniel Fast. People who partake in this fast eat mainly fruits and vegetable while avoiding animal products, food additives, refined carbohydrates, preservatives, fizzy drinks, sweets, sugar, and fast foods. Restricting the diet to only fruits and vegetables makes the Daniel Fast a low calorie diet. Besides the dietary benefits of fruits and vegetables, the low caloric state has its own benefits. As the body goes through the period of starvation, it enters into a repair mode through a process called "autophagy." This process will be explained in more detail in chapter 5. It is not surprising that people who fast live longer than those who do not fast. Though these discoveries are relatively new to science, they have been in the Bible for hundreds of years. If you study the life of Christ you will realize that it was characterized by prayer and fasting. As a consequence, he never had any health problems. That is why he makes fasting obligatory for his followers. Many Christians from different denominations across the world participate in the twenty-one-day Daniel Fast every year. This practice is taken from the book of Daniel in the Bible. It is a very good spiritual discipline and God has shown his faithfulness to those who partake in this fast. Many people have experienced breakthroughs in their lives. The duration of the Daniel Fast, as stated previously, is twenty-one days; however, there are other types of fasting with different durations. Before focusing on the Daniel Fast, let us briefly analyse the other fasts. The longest fast in

xiii

the Bible is a forty-day fast by Moses, Elijah and Jesus. During this period, they go into complete starvation, neither eating food nor drinking water. Within physiological limits, it is possible for human beings to survive without eating for forty days, as long as they are drinking water. It is beyond our physiological limits to fast this long without water unless there is divine intervention by the Holy Spirit. Determination and willpower alone are not enough without godly intervention. Many well-meaning Christians, including pastors, have died while attempting the forty-day dry fast. With water, however, the human body is capable of surviving a fast even beyond forty days. There are documented cases of this: for example, a hunger strike victim died after sixty-three days of fasting. By that time, his BMI was only 12.3 kg/m^2. The lowest BMI considered compatible with life is 12 kg/m^2. Additionally, in 1981, there was a well-publicized case of a Northern Ireland prisoner who went on a hunger strike. He was on the news daily, and the world watched as he became thinner and thinner. He died after seventy-three days of fasting.

    The number of days a person can survive during a fast is dependent on body weight. Obese people can survive longer than lean people because they have higher energy storage in the form of adipose tissue. The longest fast recorded is three hundred eighty-two days. This person made it into the Guinness Book of Records after losing 75 percent of his initial body weight. There are, however, a number of complications linked to prolonged fasting. These include ventricular fibrillation, lactic acidosis, and vitamin and electrolyte deficiency. This could be followed by sudden death syndrome, either during the fast or while eating after the fast. Fasting is very important for spiritual growth and physical health; however, if it is done without spiritual insight and medical advice, it can be detrimental to the body. It is very important for the church to be educated about fasting. There are various examples of fasting in the Bible that serve different purposes, but the scope of this book is limited to the twenty-one-day Daniel Fast. It will cover both spiritual and physiological benefits of this fast. I will also provide biblical and scientific evidence to prove that fasting is good for spiritual growth and physical health. The science in this book is not complicated, so that even people without any scientific background can understand it. May God bless you and lead you into a deeper relationship with him as you read this book.

Chapter 1

Historical Background of the Daniel Fast

DANIEL

Daniel's story has inspired Christians for centuries. What makes his story unique is that even though he was a contemporary of both Ezekiel and Jeremiah, unlike them, he was not a full-time prophet. Instead, he was a full-time administrator. This makes Daniel's life very similar to the lives of most Christians today. Many Christians are not full-time in ministry but have daytime jobs. The day jobs take most of their time and energy; therefore, their commitment to God's work is very minimal. In contrast, Daniel was an excellent prophet as well as a very successful administrator. His administrative skills are eloquently explained in Daniel 6:3: "Now Daniel so distinguished himself among administrators and the satraps by his exceptional qualities that the king planned to set him over the whole kingdom". How did Daniel manage to excel in doing God's work, in spite of his demanding full-time job as an administrator of Babylon? He understood the benefits of putting God first. Even though he was employed by Nebuchadnezzar, he had no doubt in his mind that his main employer was God. So in everything that he did as an administrator, he sought to please God. In pleasing God, Nebuchadnezzar was pleased in the process.

God's standards are very high. Any Christian who works according to God's standards is able to excel in anything they do.

What distinguishes Daniel from modern-day Christians is that he was driven by an ardent desire to please God in everything he did. He applied exceptional standards to his work because he understood that God does not bless laziness. He also did his work carefully, with diligence and trustworthiness: "They could not find any corruption in him, because he was trustworthy and neither corrupt nor negligent" (Dan 6:4). On the other hand, modern Christians do God's work half-heartedly with negligence. They are driven by the desire for material success, and since God's work does not provide any immediate material rewards, it takes a back seat. They love God and they are committed to doing his work but they love their material comforts even more. They spend most of their time accumulating material possessions with very little time for God. By not putting God first, they have unwittingly involved themselves in modern day idolatry. Wealth is their god; therefore they serve creation and not the Creator. As creatures that are created to worship God, this idol worship leaves them empty and unfulfilled. They try to close this void by working even harder to get promotions, or work overtime to get more money, with the hope that this will bring more wealth and contentment. Consequently, this gives them even less time for God's work, and the accumulated wealth just widens the void. To their dismay, big houses with large swimming pools and luxury cars do not bring contentment. In the book of Ecclesiastes, the speaker articulates this matter very eloquently, "Vanity of vanities, says the preacher, vanity of vanities! All is vanity" (Eccl 1:2). Indeed, living life without understanding God's purpose is absolute vanity.

There is an important lesson to be learned from Daniel's life: God blesses hard work. Daniel took his work seriously and he worked diligently. That is why God's blessing was always upon him. In the book of Deuteronomy, God says he will bless all the work of your hands (Deut 28:12). In other words, you have to work so that you can give God something to bless. God does not bless idle hands. Some Christians suffer from lack because they don't work, or they work half-heartedly. One of the most important messages Christ gave to his disciples before he ascended to heaven was, "Do business until I return." Work is one of the traits that characterize Gods kingdom. If you are still at school, your primary work is to study. If you have a job, whether as a manager, gardener, or cleaner, do it diligently to the glory of God and he will bless you. You will be the head and not the tail, you will always be at the top, never at the bottom (Deut 28:13).

THE CONQUEST OF JERUSALEM

To understand Daniel and the original context of the Daniel Fast, it is important to first expound the historical events surrounding the fast. Why did Daniel partake in the twenty-one-day fast? A clear understanding of the reasons will help us understand the original context and the spiritual significance of the fast.

In the year 605 BC, King Nebuchadnezzar conquered Jerusalem and took the Jews to exile in Babylon. God was punishing his people for their unfaithfulness. Despite numerous warnings by Jeremiah and other prophets, they continued with their idolatry, worshipping foreign gods. Idol worship was rampant at that time: "You have as many gods as you have towns, O Judah; and the altars you have set up to burn incense to that shameful god Baal are as many as the streets of Jerusalem" (Jer 11:13). Instead of repenting, they plotted against Jeremiah: "They said, 'Come, let's make plans against Jeremiah; for the teachings of the law by the priests will not be lost, nor will counsel from the wise, nor the word from the prophets. So come let us attack him with our tongues and pay no attention to anything he says" (Jer 18:18). When their verbal attacks did not work, they resorted to physical attacks, "When the priest Pashhur son of Immer, the chief officer in the temple of the Lord, heard Jeremiah prophesying these things, he had Jeremiah beaten and put in the stocks that were in the upper Benjamin Gate of the house of the Lord" (Jer 20:1–2). By humiliating Jeremiah, they were directly rebelling against God. As a result, God sent Nebuchadnezzar, king of Babylon, to subdue Jerusalem and capture it. Daniel witnessed the idolatry and the torture of God's prophets, and the subsequent retributive judgment of God through the hand of Nebuchadnezzar. He saw the destruction of Jerusalem by the Babylonians. He and his three friends, Hananiah (Shadrach), Mishael (Meshach), and Azariah (Abednego), were among the surviving exiles who were captured and taken to captivity in Babylon. Nothing is said about Daniel in the Bible before the exile, but from what we learn about him in Babylon, it is apparent that Daniel feared God. He clearly did not participate in the idolatry that led to the capture of Jerusalem and the destruction of the temple. That is why we see God's favor on Daniel throughout his stay in Babylon.

THE TEN-DAY VEGETABLE DIET

The king instructed Ashpenaz, the master of the eunuchs, to select young people among the Hebrew slaves who were of royal origin. They were to be skillful, intelligent, and without blemish. Among those chosen were Daniel, Shadrach, Meshach, and Abednego. They were assigned to stay in the king's palace, where they were going to be taught the language and literature of the Babylonians. They were to be fed the best palace food and wine. All of this was done to prepare them for service in the growing Babylonian empire. Though this was a very good offer, Daniel had a serious concern regarding the food, because it was not prepared according to strict Levitical laws. To avoid defiling himself, he requested that he and his three friends be given vegetables and water for ten days, instead of the succulent, mouth-watering palace food. Although Ashpenaz was reluctant at first, he finally gave in because God's favor was with Daniel, Shadrach, Meshach, and Abednego. To his amazement, after ten days, Daniel and his three friends were much healthier than the other young people who ate the palace food.

THE TWENTY-ONE-DAY VEGETABLE FAST

It is a common mistake to confuse the ten-day vegetable diet with the twenty-one-day fast. The two are different events that occur in two different time periods in history. Daniel and his friends take part in the ten-day vegetable diet at the beginning of the exile, when they had just arrived from Jerusalem. The twenty-one-day fast takes place at the end of the exile. The two events are separated by approximately seventy years. Also, each event focuses on different things. The main focus of the ten-day diet was the health benefits of a vegetable diet, while the twenty-one-day fast focuses on spiritual warfare. Nevertheless, since the twenty-one-day fast applies the principles of the vegetable diet, physical health becomes an integral part of the twenty-one-day fast.

What prompted Daniel to embark on the twenty-one-day fast? The reason for the fast is explained in the first verse of chapter 10. Daniel saw a vision about a great and terrible war that left him very distressed. He stresses over the impact of what he sees in verse 16: "I am overcome with anguish because of the vision" (Dan 10:16). We are not told much about the vision before the angel explains it, except that it concerned a great war. As a man who had walked with God for most of his life, he knew that only God can explain the mystery of this vision. He had witnessed how God rescued him and the other wise men of Babylon when God gave him an explanation to Nebuchadnezzar's dream. He had seen God rescue his friends from the fiery furnace, and the hand of God was also upon him when he was thrown into a den of lions. So he knew without a shadow of a doubt that God will clarify this mystery. He then entered into the twenty-one-day fast to seek God's wisdom regarding the vision of the great war. On the twenty-second day, an angel of the Lord arrived to clarify Daniel's vision. However,. before explaining the vision, the angel first explained why it took him twenty-one-days to bring the answer. He assured Daniel that God heard his prayer on the first day of his fast, and he responded by sending him (the angel) with an answer, but demonic forces resisted him. On the twenty-first day, the archangel Michael came to his rescue. With Michael's help, he overcame the demonic forces and managed to bring Daniel the answer. The explanation of the vision covers three chapters (10, 11, and 12) of the book of Daniel. From the angel's explanation of the vision, it is clear why Daniel was so distressed. The vision was about wars that would take place during the third and second century BC. All those events happened as predicted in Daniel's vision. However, some of the events explained by the angel have not yet happened. They include the rise of the anti-Christ, the tribulation period, the resurrection of the dead, and the final judgment. Finally the angel assured Daniel that none of the events in the vision will take place during his time. The climax of this angelic encounter comes when the angel reveals God's final plan of salvation for those who trust in him: "Everyone whose name is found written in the book of life will be delivered" (Dan 12:1). Then the message is specific to Daniel, "But go your way till the end. You will rest, and then at the end of the days you will rise to receive your allotted inheritance" (Dan 12:13).

Chapter 2

Eating Is the Original Sin

WHY WAS FASTING SO essential to Old Testament Hebrews like Daniel? Why was it such an indispensable part of the early church saints? To answer this question, we have to first understand the original sin. Since the original act of sinning that separated us from God was eating, God instituted fasting, which is the opposite of eating as an act of obedience that brings us closer to him. Before this sin of disobedience, everything was perfect. This flawlessness is narrated very well in the book of Genesis: "In the beginning God created the heavens and the earth" (Gen 1:1). Then he proceeds to create everything else, including preparing a paradise in the Garden of Eden where he placed the pinnacle of his creation, mankind, whom he created in his own image. So, unlike other created beings, including angels, mankind enjoys a unique feature of being created in God's image. God also blesses mankind and gives him his mandate: "Be fruitful and multiply and fill the earth and subdue it and have dominion over the fish of the sea and the birds of the heavens and over everything that moves on the face of the earth" (Gen 1:28). Mankind enjoys perfect fellowship with God until this relationship is destroyed by a serpent in chapter 3 of the book of Genesis. This leads to the Fall and the curse. But it is important to understand that before the Fall, mankind was blessed with fruitfulness and dominion.

Why did Adam surrender everything because of the serpent? He does not seem to offer any resistance when the snake tempts him. His wife Eve seems to offer a bit of resistance. It is important to note that the serpent does not use the name of God, Jehovah (Lord) throughout his conversation with Eve. This should have alerted Adam to the evil nature and dangerous intentions of the snake. Was the serpent more powerful than Adam, causing him to have a limited ability to resist? Did the snake have special powers to incapacitate Adam and therefore render him helpless? When God created everything he said, "It is good"; this goodness also included the nature of Adam. This means Adam had no inclination to evil, because he had never been exposed to evil. With this good nature, why was he attracted to the evil that was offered by the snake? In the next sections, we will investigate these questions and verify, using biblical doctrine to explain the Fall, that we (as Adam's seed) need to fast.

THE ORIGINAL SIN

When Adam sinned in the Garden of Eden by eating from the tree of knowledge of good and evil, his sin permeated all mankind. This can be supported by a number of scriptures both in the Old and New Testament. Paul says, "Therefore . . . sin entered the world through one man, and death through sin, and in this way death came to all men, because all sinned" (Rom 5:12) and David says, "Surely I was sinful at birth, sinful from the time my mother conceived me" (Ps 51:5). Though the doctrine of the original sin is based on a number of Bible verses, it is the story of Genesis that gives a detailed account.

TEMPTATION AND THE FALL

The first chapter of Genesis gives a narration of how God created the universe, animals, and mankind. The second chapter focuses on the relationship between God and mankind, highlighting the special commandment that God gives to mankind not to eat from the Tree of Knowledge of Good and Evil. God also explains that if they eat from this tree they will die. Then in the third chapter a talking serpent appears in the garden. Initially, the nature of the snake and the danger it poses is not clear. However when it misquotes God's command, its nature and intentions are slowly revealed. God's command was, "You are free to eat from any tree in the garden; but you must not eat from the tree of the knowledge of good and evil, for when you eat of it you will surely die" (Gen 2:16–17), but the snake said, "Did God really say, 'You must not eat from any tree in the garden?"(Gen 3:1). Then the true nature of the snake as the devil is revealed when he contradicts God's warning, "You will not surely die" (Gen 3:4). He then gives them a false promise that their eyes will be opened and they will be like God. Adam and Eve chose to disobey God by eating the fruit.

THE ROLE OF THE FREE WILL IN THE FALL

Since man was created in the image of God, he reflected the excellence and nobility of his creator. Hence there is a serious incongruity between this perfect uncorrupted being and the sin of disobedience in the Garden of Eden. By nature, Adam had no corruption within himself that prompted him toward disobedience. His inclination was completely toward good. This means after the devil presented the temptation, Adam had an easy choice of obeying God by virtue of his perfect nature. Then why did Adam opt for a more difficult choice of disobedience? To answer this question we have to understand the critical role played by the free will in the fall of mankind.

God has sovereign control over all things in creation, including mankind, but in his divine choice, he gave Adam free will. In order for free will to be truly free, it had to be neutral, neither inclined toward good or evil. Even though Adam was by nature good, his neutral free will enabled him to choose between good and evil. Before the Fall, his free will was uncorrupted and he had always used it to choose good over evil. For example, when the snake approached Eve, she was next to the forbidden fruit. This means both of them had proximity and unlimited access to the forbidden fruit and could have chosen to eat it anytime. The possibility to eat the fruit was there even before the appearance of the snake. Then why did they not eat the fruit? Their good uncorrupted nature enabled them to use their free will to choose obedience (not eating the forbidden fruit) over disobedience (eating the forbidden fruit).

To understand the true nature of Adam's sin, we have to look at how the last Adam, Jesus Christ, used his free will when he was tempted by the devil. We cannot state with certainty that Christ was like Adam before the Fall, because there is no biblical evidence for this. We are sure that Jesus was a perfect man, unblemished by sin. Therefore, the scenario in the mountain where Jesus was tempted is similar to the scenario in the garden where Adam was tempted. The narration of Jesus' temptation is found in Matthew 4:1–11. When the devil tempts him, Jesus uses his sinless good nature to overcome the devil. Like Jesus, Adam was not limited or incapacitated in any way by the devil. He had a full ability to use his free will for good instead of evil. His sinless good nature enabled him to obey God because it was not incapacitated. So his decision to eat the forbidden fruit was a conscious, deliberate act of disobedience that was in contrast to his good, uncorrupted nature. Unlike mankind after the Fall, who sin because of their inherent sinful nature, Adam had to overcome his intrinsic sinless nature to commit sin. Simply put, it was easier for Adam to obey God than to sin, hence God's severe punishment.

IMPACT OF THE FALL ON THE RELATIONSHIP BETWEEN GOD AND MANKIND

Adam's sin had a negative impact on his relationship with God. He starts hiding from God. When God calls for Adam and says, "Where are you?" (Gen 3:9), God was fully aware of Adam's physical location. He was not seeking to establish his spatial, but rather his eternal, location. Before Adam committed sin, he was eternal, but sin transformed him into a temporal being. He ceased to exist in God's eternal dimension as result of spiritual death. Though the spiritual death was immediate, his physical death was a slow and gradual process. With each passing year his organs slowly wasted away until they completely shut down and he died physically.

THE RESULT OF THE FALL WAS TOTAL DEPRAVITY

Adam's sin was very pervasive; it transcended the confines of space-time and permeated all mankind across the ages. The result of this sin is total depravity of mankind. It is important to clarify that "total depravity" refers to man's potential and not his actions. This means that even though man is totally depraved, his actions never reach the full potential of his evil nature. What stops man's depravity from reaching its full potential is not man himself, but God's common grace. Total depravity also means that the person's entire being is corrupted, including the free will. This means after the Fall, man's free will did not remain neutral but was inclined toward evil. With a corrupted nature and will, man was blind to spiritual things. He had neither the ability nor the desire to seek God or the things of God, but his entire inclination was toward evil. Given a choice between good and evil, man would choose evil. In this depraved state, man has no power within himself to come to God unless God enables him. Paul also alludes to this, "The sinful mind is hostile to God. It does not submit, nor can it do so" (Rom 8:7). Without God's initiative, mankind would be lost forever.

SPIRITUAL AND PHYSICAL RESTORATION THROUGH FASTING

After creation, one of the important instructions God gives to mankind is a dietary plan, "Behold I have given you every plant yielding seed that is on the face of the earth, and every tree with seed in its fruit. You shall have them as food" (Gen 1:29). This theme is repeated in next chapter: "And the Lord God planted a garden in Eden, in the east, and there he put the man whom he had formed. And out of the ground the Lord God made to spring up every tree that is pleasant to the sight and good for food" (Gen 2:8). In the third chapter of Genesis, we see mankind defying God's dietary instructions by eating what God had instructed them not to eat, thus committing the first sin.

Since the original sin of disobedience involved eating, abstaining from food is a means of physical and spiritual restoration for those who are in Christ. This principle does not apply outside the redemptive work of Christ. Only those who are justified by the blood of Christ can obtain spiritual restoration through fasting. Spiritual restoration in this context means being filled with the Holy Spirit, in order to be empowered to walk in the Spirit. One of the ways of being filled with the Holy Spirit is fasting. The benefit of fasting is not only limited to spiritual restoration, but also includes physical restoration. As we fast, we get very close to the perfect nature of first Adam before the Fall that was without sickness and disease. That nature is very similar to that of the last Adam who was able to carry our infirmities on the cross because of his sinless nature. The next chapters will give a detailed account of how fasting restores us physically.

Chapter 3

What to Do During the Fast

THE DANIEL FAST HAS a dual purpose, as it has spiritual and health benefits. Though most Christians get the health benefits, very few experience the spiritual benefits. Paradoxically, without the spiritual benefits, the health benefits do not last long. Very soon after the fast people return to their bad eating habits and regain all the weight they had lost. This becomes an annual cycle, losing weight in January, then regaining it during the year and reaching peak weight in December. The next January the cycle starts all over again. Years come and go and without any breakthrough.

It is important to understand that though the twenty-one-day Daniel Fast has physiological benefits, it is essentially a spiritual exercise. The primary aim is to bring people closer to God. The book of Nehemiah provides some of the spiritual disciplines that are essential for the Daniel Fast. These spiritual exercises need to be strictly adhered to, ensuring that the Daniel Fast is not downgraded into a mere religious ritual, but remains a life-changing experience.

> Now on the twenty-fourth day of this month the people of Israel were assembled with fasting and in sackcloth, and with earth on their heads. And the Israelites separated themselves from all foreigners and stood and confessed their sins and the iniquities of their fathers. And they stood up in their place and read from the Book

of the Law of the Lord their God for a quarter of a day; for another quarter of it they made confession and worshipped the Lord their God (Neh 9:1-4).

HUMILITY

During fasting, the Israelites demonstrated humility before God by wearing sackcloth and putting earth on their heads. Unfortunately, with time, this practice was abused. People were putting sackcloth and earth on their heads as a symbol of pride. It became a means of parading their fasting before the people. That is why Jesus changed the whole system: "And when you fast, do not look gloomy like the hypocrites, for they disfigure their faces that their fasting may be seen by others. Truly, I say to you, they have received their reward" (Matt 6:16-18). Jesus saw that this display of humility on the outside (sackcloth and dust) was concealing a proud heart on the inside. Thus, Jesus changed humility from being just a physical exhibition into a deep spiritual exercise. According to Jesus, humility moves from the inside to the outside. Once the heart is humbled and self-reliance is completely lost, then a person fully depends on God. Abraham demonstrates this fully when he pleads for Sodom and Gomorrah: "Abraham answered and said, 'Behold, I have undertaken to speak to the Lord, I who am but dust and ashes'" (Gen 18:27). From his words, it is clear that Abraham acknowledges the supremacy and sovereignty of God. He knows that even though he is pleading, God has the final say in the matter. That is the kind of humble attitude God wants during fasting. Partaking in the Daniel Fast does not mean we are better Christians. We should always approach the throne of God with fear and reverence, because only a prayer from a humble heart yields positive results. That is why Jesus wanted humility to be central to fasting.

How do we practice humility during the Daniel Fast? We humble ourselves by abstaining from anything that brings self-glorification. That means that, with each action, you question your motives. If anything you are about to do or say brings glory to self, then do not do it or say it. Abstaining from arguments or quarrels is another means of humbling oneself. Whether you are right or wrong is not an issue, but dying to self is the goal. It is only when you have completely died to yourself that the power of Christ in you is fully manifested. That is the power you require to bring down strongholds. Christ says, "Blessed are the meek, for they will inherit the earth" (Matt 5:5). Then the psalmist says, "The earth is the Lord's and everything in it" (Ps 24:1). God our Father owns everything and is willing to give good things to us, his children. However, pride is an obstacle that separates us from our inheritance. There are so many promises in Scripture that never manifest practically in the lives of Christians because of pride. Pride disinherited Lucifer and transformed him into the devil. That is why God will not bless us as long as we are proud, because we will fall from grace. Practicing humility during the Daniel Fast prepares us to receive God's blessings.

HOLINESS

The word "holy" is derived from the Greek word "hagios" which can be interpreted as "dedicated to God, consecrated, morally blameless and physically pure." In Nehemiah 9, when the Israelites were fasting, they separated themselves, meaning they dedicated themselves to God. So holiness means separating yourself in order to be devoted to God completely. This enables you to maintain physical and spiritual purity. Practically, you separate yourself from things that gratify the flesh, and focus on things that feed your spirit. True fasting is not possible without holiness. No gossip should come out of your mouth, nor should you listen to gossipers. During the fast, be careful of what you do, say, or listen to. Your main focus should be on prayer, thanksgiving, worshipping, personal Bible study, listening to sermons (from the pulpit, television, DVDs, and CDs) and listening to gospel music exclusively. Things to abstain from during this period of fasting include: listening to secular music, watching television (except for sermons and gospel music), going to cinemas to watch movies, and watching soccer.

Most of these things are not sinful, but they gratify the flesh and create a lot of noise in your mind, and therefore you become insensitive to the voice of the Holy Spirit. The aim of fasting is to deprive the flesh and strengthen your spirit. This cannot be achieved by abstaining from food alone, but you have to deprive yourself of anything that gives physical pleasure.

The Lord said to Moses, "Go to the people and consecrate them today and tomorrow. Have them wash their clothes and be ready by the third day. For on the third day the Lord will come down on Mount Sinai in the sight of all the people" (Exod 19:10–11). In this scenario, God was about to talk to his people and give them the Ten Commandments. For them to be able to hear God, they needed to be holy by consecrating themselves. This is still fully applicable in our context. During the Daniel Fast we have to consecrate ourselves so that we can hear from God. Sadly, most Christians have mastered the discipline of abstaining from food and eating fruits and vegetables for twenty-one days, but they have not mastered the discipline of consecration. Therefore, they get all the physiological benefits of the twenty-one day fast, but they miss the spiritual benefits. Eating fruits and vegetables is not an end in itself, but a means to an end. The ultimate purpose of the Daniel Fast is to be close to God, so consecration has to be an integral part of fasting. We have to be so close to God during the twenty-one days that after the fast we reflect God's glory, so that, like Moses, people can see that we have spent time with God.

STANDING

"Finally, be strong in the Lord and his mighty power. Put on the full armor of God so that you can take your stand against the devil's schemes. For our struggle is not against flesh and blood, but against principalities, against powers, against rulers of the darkness of this world, against spiritual wickedness in high places. Therefore put on the full armor of God, so that when the day of evil comes, you may be able to stand your ground, and after you have done everything, stand" (Eph 6:10–13). The Israelites separated themselves from other nations and stood. Standing in your position of holiness is very important during the Daniel Fast. Many challenges and temptations will come your way but you have to resist them by standing. Jesus demonstrated this when he was fasting for forty days and forty nights. The devil came to tempt him, but he stood his ground. The temptation was so difficult that angels had to minister to him after the fast. Similarly you are going to face some tough temptations during the fast. You will be faced with situations that will push you to compromise, but you must not yield. During this period you will be invited to parties and functions and offered the best meals; stand firm. People will irritate you to try to force you into arguments; stand firm. Friends will bring you the latest and juiciest gossip; stand your ground by walking away. Temptations will come in different sizes, well-packaged by the devil; do not retreat or surrender. God will reward you abundantly for standing your ground.

PRAYER

During the twenty-one-day Daniel Fast, it is normal practice for most Christians to abstain from food while continuing with their normal daily activities. They will watch soap operas and gossip as usual. When it's five-minutes-before-six in the evening, they lock themselves in the bedroom and pray for five minutes. This cycle continues for the twenty-one-day fasting period. When their daily five-minute prayers are not answered, they get angry with God. The truth is, they were not standing in prayer during the fast. Prayer should form the foundation of the fast. Every available opportunity should be used for prayer. For those who are still in school, college, or varsity, do not use your break to socialize with friends, but find a private place and pray. Those who are working have to convert their tea times and lunchtimes to prayers times. During this period, you have to pray like you have never prayed before. Prayer is a command—hence we are encouraged to pray continuously: "Pray without ceasing" (1 Thess 5:17). There are different types of prayer in the Bible that you can practice during twenty-one-day fast.

Petition Prayer

Petition prayer is when you ask God for something, or for a particular outcome. It can be about a dire financial situation, health, or family problems. Most Christians are afraid of this type of prayer because they think it's selfish. Jesus encourages us to ask, "Ask and it will be given to you; seek and you will find; knock and the door will be opened to you" (Matt 7:7). God already knows what you need but he will not give you anything unless you ask. He only acts in response to prayer. James puts it explicitly: "You have not because you ask not" (Jas 4:2). So during this twenty-one-day period, do not be afraid to ask God for whatever you need.

When we pray, God answers our prayer immediately, but the results may not manifest immediately because of the spiritual warfare. Daniel's story is a good example. The angel explains to him that God heard his prayer on the first day Daniel prayed. When the angel was bringing Daniel's answer, the prince of Persia withstood him for twenty-one days until the archangel Michael came to his assistance. So we must not give up if we do not see immediate results but we must be persistent. As we persist in prayer, angels are released to fight the spiritual warfare on our behalf. In the Bible, this battle was always won by the forces of good. Michael has never lost a battle against demonic forces. When we pray persistently, the strongholds will crumble, and we will receive all the blessings that the Father has in store for us.

Intercessory Prayer

This is when you pray on behalf of someone. The person may or may not be able to pray for himself or herself. You just stand in the gap and plead for God's favor on their behalf. This is not only limited to individuals, but it is an opportunity to pray for the government, the church, and your family. During intercession, we also plead on behalf of our friends and family members who are not saved, that they may receive the gift of salvation. Paul gives a good example of intercessory prayer: "I thank God every time I remember you, always in every prayer of mine making requests for you all with joy" (Phil 1:3–4). Intercession must be part of our twenty-one-day fast so that we do not just pray for ourselves but we also pray for others.

Prayer of Agreement

Jesus introduces us to the prayer of agreement in the book of Matthew: "Again I tell you that if two of you on earth agree about anything you ask for, it will be done for you by my Father in heaven" (Matt 18:19). Jesus teaches a principle that God honors his children's agreements. With this type of prayer, it is important to enter into an agreement with a person or people you trust. The issue you agree on could be a personal issue or a group issue. For example, a group of young adults could enter into a prayer of agreement about marriage, or a group of people with diabetes could enter into a prayer of agreement to break the disease's stronghold. A family could enter into a prayer of agreement about certain generational strongholds, like diseases or poverty.

This has three important aspects. Firstly the item on the prayer agenda must be clearly defined, e.g. marriage, sickness, finances, etc. Secondly the prayer partners must be carefully selected— for example, a friend, one's family, or fellow church members. Finally, the prayer partners must enter into an agreement to pray for the entire twenty-one-day fasting period. As they enter into this agreement, God is their witness. A person can be part of more than one prayer group. This is one of the most effective prayer methods, and its results are amazing because God honors these agreements.

Prayer of Consecration

In the beginning of every year, people are filled with aspirations and have plans. They make resolutions about changes they want to make in their lives or things they wish to accomplish. Without God, all our plans and aspirations come to nought. That is why the prayer of consecration must be part of the twenty-one-day Daniel Fast. For twenty-one days, we dedicate all our plans and aspirations to God and ask for his divine guidance. We can also consecrate ourselves to God, dedicating ourselves to his service for the year, committing our lives to him that he may use us for his purpose, in accordance to his will and for his pleasure. Hannah demonstrates this when she dedicates Samuel to God: "As surely as you live my lord, I am the woman who stood here besides you praying to the Lord. I prayed for this child and the Lord has granted me what I asked of Him. So now I give him to the Lord. For his whole life he will be given over to the Lord" (1 Sam 1:25–28).

READING THE WORD

In the ninth chapter of the book of Nehemiah, the Israelites read the Book of the Law for a quarter of the day during their fast. In our context, this may not be possible for most people because they have to go to work during the twenty-one-day fasting period. This teaches us that reading Scripture should be a daily activity that forms an essential part of your fasting. To spend enough time reading the word will require you to sacrifice certain activities that are part of your normal life. Most of the activities that have to be set aside during this period include entertainment. The time you spend watching television, going to movie theaters, or going to the stadium to watch sports could be invested in reading the word.

FAITH

During the fast you have to stand in faith. The devil will bring a lot of doubts in your mind, but do not succumb; stand in faith. Even if what you are asking for in prayer seems too big, too impossible, continue praying and do not doubt. Remember, impossibility is the chance for God. Stand in faith and keep reminding yourself that nothing is impossible with God. During fasting, you transcend the realm of the natural and you enter into the supernatural.

The supernatural is the realm of impossibilities, so do not allow the enemy's seeds of doubt to find root in your mind. Be focused. Decide on your prayer items. No matter how impossible they are, stand on your faith. Then ask God and believe you have received by faith. Even if the situation around you has not changed, believe that God has answered your prayer. Remember, when you have entered in the realm of fasting, you are no longer moved by what you see but by what God says in his word.

FAITHFULNESS

Many people do not complete the twenty-one-day fast because they lack faithfulness. During his fast, Christ's faithfulness was tested. The devil asked him to turn stones to bread and eat. I am sure this was a very tempting proposition, because he had not eaten for a long time, but he remained faithful to his Father's course. Without faithfulness, it is impossible to complete the twenty-one-day fast. When meat cravings develop, most people break the fast unceremoniously. Craving is the number-one enemy to maintaining a vegetable diet. Meat has many health problems that are outlined in the next chapters. That is why God fed the Israelites a meat-free diet when they crossed the desert. The manna kept them healthy and disease-free. But they yielded to their craving for meat and started complaining, demanding meat from God, and he gave it to them. They ate it until it choked them and came out of their nostrils, and many of them died. By remaining faithful to a strictly vegetable diet you are able to resist your cravings, even after the fast. Not only do you overcome meat cravings, but you also overcome other cravings that are harmful to the body, like sweets, unhealthy snacks, soda, fast foods, alcohol, etc. So, by remaining faithful to the Daniel Fast through following the strict dietary and spiritual program, you will be rewarded with the spiritual and physiological (health) benefits of the twenty-one-day fast.

CONFESSION OF PERSONAL SINS

Unconfessed sin is a serious hindrance to prayer. Many prayers remain unanswered because of unconfessed sin. If sin is unconfessed, it has power over the person who committed it, because it gives the devil hold over that individual. Confessing sin has a number of benefits; it brings awareness of our sinful nature, making us appreciate God's grace, and it also allows us to move sin from the subconscious mind to the conscious mind. This allows us to overcome sin through the help of the Holy Spirit, who sanctifies us. It is important to first confess your sin before God and ask for his forgiveness, and then you can confess it to a fellow Christian who may be an elder, a pastor, or a friend. However you must be careful not to confess to someone who will judge and condemn you.

CONFESSION OF GENERATIONAL SINS

The importance of confessing the sins of your ancestors is to break generational curses that may have passed on from generation to generation. These are sins that were committed by your parents and grandparents when you were young or even before you were born. Most traditions and customs involve idolatry. When children are born, it is common practice to perform rituals dedicating children to an ancestral spirit. This opens a channel for demonic spirits that bring all sorts of curses to the family, like the spirits of divorce, poverty, sickness, etc. During his fast, Daniel prays for the sins of his father: "O Lord, according to all your righteous acts, let your anger and wrath turn away from your city Jerusalem, your holy hill. Because of our sins, and for the iniquities of our fathers, Jerusalem and your people have become a byword among all who are around us" (Dan 9:16). By confessing the sins of your fathers, you break the vicious cycle and you bring down the strongholds against your family.

WORSHIPPING

The purpose of worship is to glorify God. Therefore, worship must form an integral part of the twenty-one-day Daniel Fast. When we worship, the Holy Spirit intercedes on our behalf. Paul articulates this well in Romans 8:26–27: "Likewise, the Spirit helps us in our weakness. For we do not know what to pray for as we ought, but the Spirit Himself intercedes for us with groanings too deep for words. And He who searches hearts knows what is the mind of the Spirit, because the Spirit intercedes for the saints according to the will of God." Therefore, as we worship, the Spirit presents our prayers as a good fragrance before God. It is important at this point to state that worship is more than singing songs and lifting hands during a church service. True worship is about presenting yourself before God as a living sacrifice. Christ expresses it very well in John 4:21: "Neither on this mountain nor in Jerusalem will you worship the Father." This means worship is not limited to a physical space, like a church building, but is a continuous activity in a life of a Christian. The corporate worship that we partake in during a Sunday service is only a small part of worship. We have to learn to worship the Father in spirit and in truth, as Jesus says: "God is spirit, and those who worship must worship in spirit and truth" (John 4:24). Worship must go beyond the Sunday church service and permeate our lives throughout the week. If there is a disconnect between our Sunday worship and the lifestyle we live during the week, then we are not true worshippers. For us to be true worshippers, our Sunday worship must be complemented by our lifestyle outside the church. Everything we do must be an act of worship. The way we behave at work or school, the way we treat others, even the way we speak must bring glory to God. This is vital because it allows us to fulfill what Christ teaches in Matthew 5:16: "Let your light so shine before others, that they may see your good works and glorify your Father who is in heaven." When our daily activities bring glory to God, then we are the true worshippers that the Father is looking for.

Why do we fast? The first answer to this question is very simple and straightforward. We fast because Jesus commands us to. So when we fast, we are simply obeying Christ. However, we can take this question to another level. Why did Christ command us to fast? The answer to this question is much deeper than the first, because it requires us to understand the mind of God. Sadly, that is an impossible task because no one can understand God unless he reveals himself. Therefore, since God has revealed himself in the Scriptures, we have to dig deep into the Bible to find the answer. The Bible gives us answers to some of these questions.

WALKING IN THE SPIRIT

We fast so that we can walk in the spirit. According to the Bible, a human being has a triune nature: body, spirit, and mind. These three parts have separate specialized functions which are integrated to produce a particular outcome. The spirit operates on the principles of faith, and the body operates on empirical senses like sight, taste, smell, hearing, and touch. The mind does not operate independently; it is controlled by both the spirit and the body. Whatever is stronger between the two will dominate the mind and ultimately determine the actions of an individual. Since the flesh operates only by the empirical senses, it is limited by the laws of physics, such as gravity. The spirit operates by faith so it can transcend into the supernatural, where the physical laws do not operate. Therefore, the spirit can operate in both the natural and supernatural realm. This brings us to our question: why do we fast? We fast to create disequilibrium between the spirit and the flesh. Fasting weakens the flesh and strengthens the spirit. This enables us to transcend the limitations of the flesh and tap into the supernatural. Paul makes this point very clear in 2 Cor 4:16: "So we do not lose heart. Though our outer self is wasting away, our inner self is being renewed day by day." The outer self refers to the flesh, and the inner self to the spirit. If we do not fast, then we will walk in the flesh which is already wasting away or decaying. Logically, it is clear that if we lean on something that is decaying we will surely fall. Fear, failure, and sinfulness characterize the lives of Christians who do not fast. They are limited to the natural because they are ruled by the flesh. By fasting, we empower the inner self that is already being renewed. That enables us to walk in the spirit and hence experience the fullness of Christ in our lives. Christ says he has come so that we may have life in abundance (John 10:10). We can only experience a life of abundance and overflow if we walk in the spirit through fasting.

LIVING A HEALTHY LIFESTYLE

Daniel applied the principle of putting God first in everything that he did. As soon as he arrived in Babylon, it was clear that his fate was not going to be similar to that of the other exiles. He and his three friends were taken to the palace where they were going to live a life of luxury. Yet instead of indulging in the palace luxuries, he was more concerned about defiling himself. He wanted to remain ritually clean. To the twenty-first-century Christian, ceremonial cleanliness may not hold any significance, but to the Hebrews it had a very profound spiritual significance. They did not put much distinction between sin and ritual cleanliness. So to Daniel, being ritually clean was an act of worship to his God. That is why he could not indulge in the palace feasts, because some of the food that was eaten by the Babylonians was dedicated to idols.

Before doing anything, Daniel and his friends always prioritized seeking the will of God. Even in something as simple as eating, they sought the will of God. Even though they were presented with mouth-watering palace delicacies, they opted to please God and not their appetite. Because they practiced obedience in small things, they were able to obey God in the face of life-threatening challenges, like the fiery furnace and hungry lions. With Daniel's example in mind, we have to pose this challenge to ourselves as modern Christians: before eating or praying for our food, we have to look carefully at what we are about to eat and ask ourselves some questions. Is God pleased with what I am about to eat? Is the artery-clogging fat in my plate, the processed starch, or the sugar in my fizzy drink pleasing to God? If the answer is no, then you have to change your eating habits and align them to God's word. Remember every time you eat that your body is the temple of the Holy Spirit, therefore you cannot poison it with unhealthy food. Obedience to God should dictate what we eat. The Daniel Fast teaches the discipline of healthy living. If you learn to be obedient in what you eat, then like Daniel and his friends you will be able to withstand bigger life challenges. You will also be free from most lifestyle diseases and live an enjoyable, healthy life.

SENSITIVITY TO THE VOICE OF THE HOLY SPIRIT

God spoke to Daniel at regular intervals in different ways, such as dreams, visions, and angels. His life had direction and purpose because he had constant instruction from God. This practice of prayer and fasting in order to get clear directives from the Holy Spirit was also practiced in the early church. A typical example is found in chapter 13 of the book of Acts: "While they were worshipping the Lord and fasting, the Holy Spirit said, "Set for me aside Barnabas and Saul for the work for which I have called them." This clear instruction came while they were fasting, because during the fast their spirits were very sensitive to the gentle voice of the Holy Spirit. We generally miss this gentle voice, because we live in a busy world that is full of noises that clog our spiritual ears. Only fasting brings the quietude that empowers us to decipher the voice of the Holy Spirit. That is why it is important to be holy during the fasting period. Holiness guarantees that physical as well as spiritual noises are silenced. Sources of these noises include entertainment like watching TV soap operas, soccer, rugby, football, baseball, movies, and listening to non-gospel music. These activities are not necessarily sinful, but they have no spiritual benefit. They just gratify the flesh while draining the spirit, because they steal time from prayer, worship, and reading the word. During fasting, the flesh must be deprived of both food and entertainment. If only food is deprived, the flesh will not be weakened because it will compensate by getting all the energy it needs from entertainment. A typical example is a Christian who abstains from food but spends the whole day watching soccer or movies on television. When time comes to break the fast (usually 6 p.m.), they make a quick five-minute prayer and start eating. Nothing is received from the Holy Spirit because of all the noise echoing from the entertainment. Sadly, this is the most common type of fasting in the modern church. Pastors and church leaders spend more time in front of their television sets than on their knees. As a result, the church operates on human ideas and not on the directives of the Holy Spirit. The infighting, jostling for positions, and lack of spiritual growth are all features of a church that does not submit to the headship of Christ. The noises that pastors and leaders allow to permeate our spiritual space during fasting have disconnected the Head (Christ) from the body and completely alienated the Holy Spirit. Lack of spiritual direction in the church is a clear indication that the Holy Spirit has departed from most pulpits. The church today is in desperate need of pastors and leaders who will fast in silence until they hear the voice of the Holy Spirit.

RECEIVING AFFIRMATION FROM GOD

After fasting for twenty-one days, Daniel is visited by an angel, and the first words the angel speaks to Daniel are words of affirmation: "O Daniel, man greatly loved" (Dan 10:10). On hearing these words, Daniel is strengthened. Sometimes the challenges that we go through in this life leave us drained and tired. We even lose sight of the fact that God loves us. In that state we are very vulnerable to the trickeries of the devil. That is why, every once in a while, we need affirmation from God. Even though we know that he loves us, we still need constant assurance. It always feels good to receive direct affirmation from God. It is a life-transforming experience. When Gideon received it, he was transformed from self-debasing coward into a hero that liberated Israel from Median oppression. When the angel of the Lord said to Gideon, "The Lord is with you, O mighty man of valor", there was nothing heroic about Gideon at that time. Actually, he was busy hiding his wheat from the Midianites. Yet in the midst of this cowardly act God sees a man of valor. Clearly God's perception of who we are is not cluttered by our actions and circumstances. He is able to focus through the clutter and see the good deposit he has invested in us. Unfortunately, we have allowed fellow human beings to define who we are and their perceptions of who we are mainly governed by our actions and circumstances. Based on your race, gender, family background, educational status, and economic status, people define us and package us into well-labeled boxes. We fit ourselves comfortably in these boxes, limiting ourselves to the world inside, never venturing to look outside its borders. We are not even aware that we live in the box because to us, the box is the entire universe. Like our boxes, Gideon's box was well-labeled. He describes the box very well in his own words: "Please, Lord, how can I save Israel? Behold, my clan is the weakest in Manasseh, and I am the least in my father's house" (Judg 6:15). He lived inside a box with a three-layered wall. The first layer was his nation. The Hebrews at that time were a very weak people that were bullied by the Midianites and the Amalekites. These two nations would make unscheduled visits to the land of the Israelites and take all their sustenance; i.e. their crops, oxen, and donkeys. The Israelites starved because they were weak and defenseless against these nations. Gideon was part of that national tragedy. The second layer was his clan. This can be equivalent to a surname in our context. His clan was the weakest in the house of Manasseh. It had not contributed anything significant to the history of Manasseh. It had no war heroes. There are similar examples in the church today. There are people who are disregarded in the church today because their surnames are not prominent in the church. There are no famous evangelists or pastors with that surname in the church history. Even if these individuals work hard in the church they are never recognized by the leadership. They are the no-name brands of the church. No one notices when they miss a church service. That was Gideon's situation. Finally, the third layer was his position in the family. He was an insignificant child, the one who would try to contribute to a family discussion and everyone would break out in laughter, ridiculing him. His parents probably did not invest much time in him because nothing important was expected from him. His only speciality was beating the wheat and hiding it. This was his box. He was safe inside this box because as long as he was inside this box no one would hurt him. The depth of his scars becomes apparent when God calls him to action. In his jaded mind he thinks it's another prank call that is intended to remove him from his comfort box so that he can be ridiculed and hurt. Even when God assures him, "But I will be with you and you will strike the Midianites as one man" (6:16), he refuses to believe. How can an insignificant non-entity who lives in a box strike down the Midianites as one man? Surely this couldn't be God. God knew that there are heroes in Israel who were up to that task. So it must be another joke. Exposing jokes was one of his hidden talents. This skill had saved him from humiliation and hurt in the past. Yet God's affirmation struck a chord that had never been struck in his life before. He tries to crawl back into his box, but the box becomes uncomfortable because the chord's resonates in his spirit. In spite of his pain and scepticism, deep down he knows God touched him. Unable to suppress the waves of affirmation, he asks God for a sign as a confirmation: "If now I have found favor in your eyes, then show me a sign that it is you who speaks with me." God honors his request and gives him the sign. His shock as he witnesses the miracle shows that he truly did not believe this was God all along: "Alas, O Lord God! For now I have seen the angel of the Lord face-to-face" (Judg 6:22). At that moment he steps out of his box and God uses him mightily. He overcomes his family strongholds that have limited him from the moment he was born, he breaks through the limitations of his clan that had subdued him to obscurity, and he becomes the ultimate national hero that liberates the whole of Israel.

Many Christians live mediocre lives, barely breaking above average and always scraping at the bottom. Whatever they try to do fails because they are boxed. The walls of their box are a solid concrete of their poor family background, unemployment, inherited diseases, deteriorating national economy, divorce, etc. The solution that can bring down these walls is God's affirmation that can only be perceived when we fast. This does not mean that God does not affirm us when we are not fasting. God is constantly affirming us, but because of the background noise in our busy lives, we cannot perceive the voice of the Holy Spirit. When affirmation is not perceived, it does not strike a chord, and the mighty valor remains locked up quiescently. There are certain strengths that will continue to lay dormant in us until God's affirmation illuminates them. When we fast, we are brought into the tranquility of God's presence, his words of affirmation resonate loudly, and we hear them as they echo over and over again in our spirit:

- You who are greatly beloved
- Man of valor
- You are more than a conqueror
- With you nothing will be impossible

With the affirmation comes the strength to stand in the midst of trials and tribulation. That is why it is important to partake in the Daniel Fast, especially in January. Beginning the year with God's affirmation prepares you to take hold of that which God has in store for you for the year ahead.

PURSUING GOD'S AGENDA

On New Year's Eve or New Year's Day, most Christians make resolutions for the New Year. Sadly, these resolutions are made without a clear understanding of God's agenda. Our God is a God of purpose. His purposes stretch from the invisible spiritual realm to the entire universe, and to individual human beings. Our lives can only have meaning if they are lived according to God's purpose. Hence, it is important to know God's agenda for our lives. Fasting brings us closer to God and enables us to hear the voice of the Holy Spirit; he outlines God's agenda for our lives. Each time we fast, God's agenda for our lives becomes clearer.

BREAKING STRONGHOLDS

Some of the painful and distressing experiences in life are not just trials, but they are strongholds. The difference between the two is that trials are not permanent. They last for a certain period, then they pass. Their aim is to help us grow spiritually by bringing us closer to God. James puts this very eloquently: "Consider it pure joy, my brothers, whenever you face trials of many kinds, because you know that the testing of your faith develops perseverance. Perseverance must finish its work so that you may be mature and complete, not lacking anything" (Jas 1:2–4). On the other hand, strongholds tend to last forever. They are not meant to develop you, but to oppress you. The word "stronghold" is found only once in the Bible. It is used by Paul in 2 Corinthians: "Though we walk in the flesh, we do not war according to the flesh, for the weapons of our warfare are not of the flesh but have divine power to destroy strongholds" (2 Cor 10:3–4). Paul interprets the metaphor of a stronghold in the next verse: "We destroy arguments and every obstacle to the knowledge of God" (2 Cor 10:5). Arguments are philosophies upon which the worldly system is based. They shape political and economic policies worldwide, creating war, poverty, and suffering throughout the world. Besides the arguments, Paul talks about obstacles that are an impediment to the knowledge of God. These are dark forces that stand against anything godly. Paul says more about these dark forces in Ephesians: "For we wrestle not against flesh and blood, but against principalities, against powers, against rulers of the darkness of this world, against spiritual wickedness in high places" (Eph 6:12). These principalities are demonic forces, and their chief commander is the devil. They are the same forces that withstood the angel who was bringing Daniel's answer. If they are not stopped, they manifest in physical strongholds like sickness, poverty, conflicts, etc. These distresses do not just last for a season, but they tend to be permanent unless they are uprooted by sustained prayer and fasting. Daniel's experience teaches us that sometimes prayer alone is not sufficient to remove these strongholds. They are so deeply rooted that we need both prayer and fasting to uproot them. Even Christ confirms this in Mark: "This kind can only come out by prayer and fasting" (Mark 9:29). Through prayer and fasting, Michael was released and he defeated the demon that was blocking Daniel's answer therefore the twenty-one-day Daniel Fast is a powerful spiritual weapon that can bring down any stronghold in our lives.

Chapter 4

Knowing God

ONE OF THE MOST important things that a Christian must accomplish during the Daniel Fast is to know God. Reading the word during the fast is the most important tool in the pursuit of the knowledge of God. According to the Bible, he is the only true one, *El Shaddai*, the Almighty God. He is the God of Genesis who created the heavens and the entire universe. He created mankind and had fellowship with him in the Garden of Eden. When his relationship with mankind was disconnected as the result of sin, he did not give up but he sought to re-establish fellowship with his creation. He put his salvation plan into action, a plan that involved him revealing himself progressively to mankind over the ages. This culminated in the revelation he made in the person of Jesus Christ.

He revealed himself to Abraham and made a covenant with him: "Leave your country, your people, and your father's household and go to the land I will show you. I will make you into a great nation and I will bless you; I will make your name great, and you will be a blessing" (Gen 12:1–2). In Exodus, the setting seems to contradict God's promise in Genesis. As promised by God, Abraham's offspring has multiplied but they are not a great nation—instead, they are Egyptian slaves. This was God's way of building them into a strong nation. We also go through difficult times in our lives that seem to contradict the promises of Scripture. Sometimes God uses adversity to build our spiritual muscles. Those who do not know God become despondent and think that God has forgotten them. God is always with his children; he never forgets them. Just as he was with Israel in Egypt, he is with his children.

The theme of progressive revelation continues in the book of Exodus. God reveals himself to Moses in Mount Horeb and sends him to Egypt to liberate the children of Israel from slavery. Moses responded with a question, "Suppose I go to the Israelites and say to them, 'The God of your fathers has sent me to you,' and they ask me, 'What is his name?' Then what shall I tell them?" (Exod 3:13). This is a fair question, considering that Moses was brought up in an Egyptian palace, so he did not know God. God understands his naivety and responds to his question in this way: "I Am Who I Am. This is what you are to say to the Israelites: 'I Am has sent me to you'" (Exod 3:14). Moses obeys and goes to Pharaoh, who responds very arrogantly: "Who is the LORD that I should obey him and let Israel go? I do not know the LORD and I will not let Israel go" (Exod 5:2). To make matters worse, Pharaoh increases the work load of the Israelites. To the carnal eye, this situation seems desperate, but this was part of God's plan. He wanted to display his power, so that when Egypt crumbles to ashes, everyone would know that it was the hand of God. Situations may get worse before they get better during the fast. During these times of trials, some Christians may give up and break the fast. Yet those who know their God hold on during these times, knowing that just as he liberated the Israelites from Egypt, he will give them their breakthrough.

God appears again to Moses, whose spirit was crushed by Pharaoh's negative response. He reveals his purpose to fulfill the covenant he made to Abraham, "I am the LORD. I appeared to Abraham, to Isaac and to Jacob as God Almighty, but by my name the LORD I did not make myself known to them. I also established my covenant with them to give them the land of Canaan, where they lived as aliens" (Exod 6:2–4). Moses responds by going back to Pharaoh, and indeed, God fulfills his promise by unleashing his power against Egypt. Pharaoh is forced to release the Israelites and the story has a happy ending. This biblical passage has raised a number of questions that will be addressed in the following paragraphs.

THE NAME OF GOD

God's response to Moses when he asked for his name is "I Am that I Am" which is the literal English translation of the Hebrew "*Ehyeh asher Ehyeh.*" "Ehyeh" is the first person singular, usually translated as "I am." Some scholars believe that from the same root, *ehye,* the tetragrammaton "YHWH" was derived. When "YHWH" was transliterated into Greek by the early Christian writers, its pronunciation became "Yahweh", from which the English hybrid "Jehovah" was derived. In most English translations, "Lord" is used instead of Jehovah. His name ("I Am that I Am," "Yahweh," "Jehovah") is a clear representation of a self-existent, eternal, uncreated, immutable Creator who is independent of anything. The name rightfully depicts God's existence in relation to his character and creation. This is the God we fellowship with when we enter into the Daniel Fast.

God told Moses that he appeared to Abraham, Isaac, and Jacob by the name "God Almighty," but by the name "the Lord" he was not known to them. This creates an impression that the name "Yahweh" was not known to the patriarchs. This seems to contradict Genesis 4:6, which says men began to call upon the name of the Lord. This name also appears when God speaks to Abraham in Genesis 15:7. He says to Abraham, "I am the Lord." It is clear that the name of God was known long before Moses' time. This is also confirmed by the way Moses phrases his question. He says, "What is his name" and not, "Who is his name." The particle *mah* (what) is interrogative. It highlights the fact that Moses was not asking for a name, but was seeking the meaning of the name. If he was only asking for the name, then he would have used the particle *mi* (who), which is normally used when simply asking for a name.

God is beyond our knowledge; we cannot discover him by ourselves. For us to know him, he must reveal himself. To get a clear understanding of what knowing God means, we need to look at the meaning of the word "know" in the Hebrew context. The Hebrew word for "know" is *yada*. In the Hebrew context, this does not merely mean "to be acquainted with," but it also means to know properly and intimately. So, knowing God is very different than knowing about God. To know God goes beyond having knowledge about God, but having an intimate relationship with him. That is why only those who spend time with him in fasting get to know him. When God says he was not known by the name "the Lord," he does not mean they did not know the name "Lord," but he is talking about a relationship. In God's first statement, "And I appeared to Abraham, Isaac and Jacob by the name of God Almighty" (Exod 6:3), this means that they knew him relationally as *El Shaddai*, the all-sufficient God who is able to fulfill his promises and covenant. Revealing himself as *El Shaddai* was a means of revealing his divine character to the patriarchs.

Abraham, Isaac, and Jacob did not witness the fulfillment of the covenant; therefore to them, he was not known as to the efficacy of the name "Yahweh." Even though they had worshipped him for years, they had never witnessed his mighty act of deliverance experienced by the Israelites in Exodus. To them he was not revealed as "Yahweh." In the Hebrew context, knowledge of the name of God is always associated with experiencing his divine character related to that name. Another practical example is in Judges: "And all that generation also were gathered to their fathers. And there arose another generation after them that did not know the Lord or the work that he had done for Israel" (Judg 2:10). In this context, it is clear that to know the Lord includes experiencing his mighty power of delivering Israel from her enemies. The second part of God's statement says, "But by my name the Lord I was not known to them." This was in reference to Moses' experience at Mount Horeb when God revealed himself as the Lord. This revelation of God's name meant that Moses was about to witness the promises that were made to Abraham. Moses was about to witness the fulfillment of the promise, hence God appeared to him as the Lord.

GOD REMEMBERS HIS COVENANT

God remembers the covenant he made to Abraham. He then outlines the seven ways he will fulfill it:

- To give them the land of Canaan
- To deliver them from slavery
- To redeem them
- To judge Egypt
- To take Israel to be his people
- To be their God
- To let them know him

When God says he remembers his covenant, it does not mean he had forgotten it. In Hebrew the word "remember" is *zakar* and it means "to mark, so as to make recognizable." This means that God was making his covenant prominent because he was about to act on it. Before fulfilling this promise, he had to remove the serious obstacle that was hindering the fulfillment of this promise. God was not known. Egypt did not know him (Exod 7:5), Pharaoh did not know him (Exod 5:2), the patriarchs did not know him (Exod 6:3), Israel did not know him (Exod 6:7), Moses did not know him (Exod 8:22). In the act of making himself known, he also fulfills the promise. He first makes himself known by judging Egypt through the ten plagues that he unleashes upon Egypt. This is followed by the exodus, and the promise is completely fulfilled when they enter the Promised Land. God still applies the same principle to us today. He must make himself known to us before he can fulfill the promises of Scripture. Though the initiative comes from God, because we cannot know him unless he reveals himself, we have to show intent of willing to know him. We show this intent by drawing close to him through fasting.

GOD'S REVELATION IS PROGRESSIVE

From the text we also learn about the progressive revelation of God. The patriarchs knew the name of God and worshipped him, but they never knew him in terms of his character and the fulfillment of his covenant. For years they worshipped God without truly knowing him. The knowledge of God does not come through mankind's initiative, but as stated in the last paragraph, we can only know God as he reveals himself. This revelation is progressive. To the patriarchs, he revealed himself *El Shaddai*. They were not a nation, then, therefore this revelation was sufficient. At Mount Horeb, the revelation goes deeper. He reveals himself as Jehovah, the eternal and self-existent God. To us this revelation is even more profound. He has revealed himself through Jesus Christ. This revelation is revolutionary, because Jesus teaches that God is our Father.

Knowing God does not mean knowing his name or knowing that he exists. It is also not just knowing about him and performing religious duties. It means to know his redemptive power. Paul states it clearly when he says, "That I may know him and the power of his resurrection" (Phil 3:10). Knowing God is not simply intellectual exercise or a mental recall of his name, but it is relational. You may know all of his names, but if you have not experienced his redemptive power through Jesus Christ, then you do not know him. In the Old Testament, God revealed himself through human agents like the patriarchs, Moses, and the prophets, but in the New Testament, he has revealed himself through his Son, Jesus Christ. The book of Hebrews confirms this: "Long ago, at many times and in many ways, God spoke to our fathers by the prophets, but in these last days he has spoken to us by his Son, whom he appointed the heir of all things, through whom also he created the world" (Heb 1:2). The New Testament has many promises—however, the condition of fulfillment of these promises is still very similar to those of the Old Testament. Before God fulfilled his promise to the Israelites, they had to know him first. Therefore, even today, before anyone can experience the practical fulfillment of God's promise in their lives, they first have to know him. That knowledge can only come through God the Son.

Through the Son's redemptive work on the cross, we are reconciled to our Father. The Holy Spirit draws us even closer to him through sanctification. We have to show intent of drawing close to him through fasting. Then God will fulfill his promises to the glory of his name. Jesus says we must seek his kingdom and his righteousness first, then all these things will be added unto us (Matt 6:33). We have to remove our focus on things and put it on God. As we plan the Daniel Fast, our first intention must be to know him, and then material blessings and health will be given to us. Just as he had a plan for the Israelites, he also has a plan for us. He redeemed them from slavery and showed them his power when he split the Red Sea. They crossed on dry land and watched as he drowned Pharaoh's army. God has also redeemed us from the bondage of sin through the blood of Jesus Christ.

We are made in the image of God, and Christ is the complete revelation of God's image. After justification, the Holy Spirit conforms us to his image. As we become more like him, his power is also manifested in us. This power is revealed to us gradually as we learn to walk in the Spirit. Even his disciples did not receive all the revelation at once. They received it gradually, and most of it was given to them after he ascended to heaven. He explained to them, "I still have many things to say to you, but you cannot bear them now. When the Spirit of truth comes, he will guide you into all truth" (John 16:12–13). This applies to us as well. As the Holy Spirit sanctifies us, conforming us to the image of Christ, God progressively reveals himself to us.

God is the same yesterday today and forever. He is immutable and omnipotent. Exodus 6:1–7 gives an example of how he is true to his word. From these verses we can learn that he is able and willing to fulfill his promises irrespective of circumstances. Pharaoh was very arrogant, and he thought he had power over the Israelites, but he did not know that his power was from God. It was given to him so that God could fulfill his purpose. He was just a pawn in God's hand. At the appointed time, God redeemed his people. Even today, we may be overwhelmed by unsurmountable problems. These can be financial, health related, etc. The omnipotent God who rescued the Israelites is still able to rescue us today. We just have to remain focused on him. Through faith we share in Abraham's blessings. We don't have to be biological descendants to share in this blessing, because real descendants are those who have faith in Jesus Christ. The promises that were made to Abraham were also intended for us.

Fasting must be practiced in its proper context, a means to draw close to God with the aim of knowing him. It must not be used as a quick-fix solution for our problems. As stated earlier, God wants to be known first before he can give his blessings. As we humble ourselves and seek his face through fasting, he reveals himself to us. It is this revelation that ushers our blessings.

Chapter 5

Why Don't We Eat Meat During the Daniel Fast?

AND GOD SAID, "BEHOLD I have given you every plant yielding seed that is on the face of all the earth, and every tree with seed in its fruit. You shall have them for food" (Gen 1:29). And the Lord God planted a garden in Eden, in the east, and there he put the man whom had formed (Gen 2:8). What is evident from these verses is that God prescribed a strict vegetarian diet for man after creation. The reason for this strict vegetarian diet was that man was created to have a very long lifespan, and fruits and vegetables have the ability to promote longevity. Even though fruits and vegetables were going to prolong mankind lifespan, they could not make mankind live forever. That is why God put the tree of life in the Garden of Eden. "You may surely eat of every tree of the garden" (Gen 2:16). From this verse we can see that God allowed man to eat of every tree in the garden, including the tree of life. The purpose of the tree of life was for healing, to ensure that mankind lives forever in good health. The only exception was the tree of knowledge of good and evil. "But of the tree of knowledge of good and evil you shall not eat, for in the day that you eat of it you shall surely die" (Gen 2:17).

In Genesis 3, we see mankind defying God's commandment by eating from the tree of knowledge of good and evil. Immediately after Adam and Eve ate from the tree, they began to die, both physically and spiritually. Spiritual death was instantaneous: "Where are you?" (Gen 3:9). God was not inquiring here about Adam's spatial location, but his spiritual orientation. The instant Adam sinned, he died spiritually, and his spiritual link to God was severed—however, he continued to live physically. To prevent mankind from living continuously in perpetual sin like the devil and his demons, God evicts Adam and his wife from the Garden of Eden so that they may not have any access to the tree of life. This was to ensure that they die physically as well: "He drove out the man, and at the east of the Garden of Eden He placed the cherubim and a flaming sword that turned every way to guard the way to the tree of life" (Gen 3:24).

MEAT SHORTENS OUR LIFESPAN

Even though human beings began to die because of lack of access to the tree of life, human lifespan was very long (hundreds of years). The person who lived the longest lifespan at that time was Methuselah, who lived nine hundred sixty-nine years. This long lifespan turned into a curse, because women were married to angels (the sons of God) and gave birth to giants called Nephilim (Gen 6:4). This was not God's plan for the earth, so he decided to reduce mankind's lifespan: "My spirit shall not abide in man forever, for he is flesh: his days shall be a hundred and twenty years" (Gen 6:3). To put this plan into action, God allows mankind to eat meat, "Every moving thing that lives shall be food for you, and as I gave you green plants, I now give you everything" (Gen 9:3). Consumption of meat resulted in the reduction of life span. The shortening of mankind's lifespan does not happen instantly, but gradually, over generations. We see this decline in lifespan when we follow the generations of the sons of Noah. Shem lived five hundred years, and generations later Terah, Abraham's father, only lived two hundred and five years. Abraham's lifespan is even shorter: one hundred seventy-five years. By the time we get to Moses, mankind's lifespan was reduced to one hundred twenty years; Moses was exactly that age when he died (Deuteronomy 34:7).

Why Don't We Eat Meat During the Daniel Fast?

When God was leading the Israelites through the desert after liberating them from Egypt, he feeds them a meat-free diet. Since they were shepherds, they must have left Egypt with their sheep and goats, yet they complain of hunger. At one point they crave meat. Why did they not eat their livestock? Even when they craved meat, he gives them bird meat instead of allowing them to slaughter and eat their livestock. Was exclusion of red meat from their diet a mere coincidence, or did God do it on purpose? We cannot answer this question with certainty, but we can make certain deductions. The manna that they ate kept them healthy throughout the challenging journey in the desert. Red meat has a lot of potential health problems that would have made their journey through the desert impossible. Studies have shown that red meat, or meat that is red before it is cooked, is not good for health. These dangers are observed when red meat is consumed regularly. The strongest evidence is the link between red meat consumption and bowel cancer. Though pancreatic cancer has also been linked to meat consumption, the evidence is not as strong. It is important to clarify at this point that the link between meat and cancer is only with red meat. Chicken, turkey, and fish have not been linked to cancer. It is therefore advisable to those who wish to pursue a long lifespan to cut down on red meat, and increase fish and vegetable consumption.

When God allows the Israelites to eat meat, it sounds like a compromise: "When the Lord enlarges your territory, as he has promised you, and you say, "I will eat meat," because you crave meat, you may eat meat whenever you desire" (Deut 12:20). This scripture confirms that they were not allowed to eat meat in the desert. They only started to eat meat when they entered the Promised Land. However, the initiative to eat meat does not seem to come from God; rather, it comes from the Israelites and it seems to be driven by cravings. The fact that meat was not prescribed by God in the Garden of Eden, nor was it allowed in the desert, means that eating meat is not God's perfect will, but rather his permissive will. Based on that understanding it is advisable for Christians to eat meat, especially red meat, with caution.

SATURATED FAT

"Thou shalt not eat fat of ox, sheep or goat" (Lev 7:21b). When the Israelites entered the Promised Land, they finally had the freedom to slaughter their cattle, sheep, and goats, but this came with an instruction not to eat animal fat. They still had to fight battles to drive out many nations out of the land. Eating fat would incapacitate them from performing this task, because they would be fat and sick. Animal fat increases body weight because of its high calorie content. Furthermore, it is saturated, and so increases the bad low density lipoprotein (LDL) cholesterol, which is a risk factor for heart diseases and strokes. God forbids the Israelites from eating fat so that they can be fit and healthy for the task of occupying the Promised Land. This is very relevant for Christians today. They are not able to carry out their God-given mandate that leads to a life of blessings due to ill health, resulting from bad eating habits. That is why it is important for Christians to partake in the Daniel Fast at least once a year. This will remind them of the biblical principles of spiritual and physical health.

HEMOCHROMATOSIS

"You shall not eat any flesh with blood on it" (Lev 19:26). Besides avoiding animal fat, permission to eat meat came with another instruction: do not eat meat with blood on it. Eating meat with a lot of blood has serious health implications. Before delving into the scientific explanation of the dangers of eating blood, let me first explain the original spiritual context. Eating blood was not allowed because blood had a significance in atonement. Atonement through the blood of animals was fulfilled by the redemptive work of Christ when he died on the cross. Now that we have explained the biblical context, we can look at the science. Blood is very rich in iron. When iron is confined inside the blood vessels as part of hemoglobin, it does not create any problems. It actually plays an essential role in the transport of oxygen. When it is consumed in large quantities in the form of blood, it becomes toxic. It causes cirrhosis of the liver, a condition called hemochromatosis.

INSULIN-LIKE GROWTH FACTOR-1 (IGF-1)

People often miss meat during the Daniel Fast. Most people are addicted to meat without knowing it. Hence, it is traditional to eat meat daily with the main meal. Meat consumption increases the insulin-like growth factor-1 (IGF-1). This protein, also known as somatostatin C, is implicated in a number of cancers. One of the cancers associated with IGF-1 is prostate cancer. Studies have shown a strong association between IGF-1 and prostate cancer. Men who consume red meat have high levels of IGF-1, which causes proliferation and growth of cancer cells. Tests for prostate cancer risk are performed by measuring levels of prostate-specific antigen (PSA) in the blood. Men with elevated levels of PSA are more likely to be diagnosed with prostate cancer, compared to men with normal levels of PSA. However, if men had high levels of IGF-1, their risk of developing prostate cancer was found to be high even though their levels of PSA were normal. This further confirms the dangers of prostate cancer in men who consume red meat regularly. Women are also not safe from the effects of IGF-1. High levels of IGF-1 are associated with an increased risk of breast cancer. IGF-1 is thought to cause the proliferation of breast cancer cells. So just like men, women who consume red meat regularly are at a higher risk of developing cancer, compared to women who consume red meat casually.

HEMOGLOBIN

Hemoglobin is the red pigment that occurs naturally in meat. It plays an important role in the transport of oxygen in the body. The oxygen that we breathe into our lungs is carried by hemoglobin to the different parts of the body where the cells use it to produce energy. People who do not have enough hemoglobin suffer from chronic fatigue because they don't have enough energy. Our bodies can synthesize their own hemoglobin; therefore, we do not depend on hemoglobin from red meat. However the iron from red meat is essential in the synthesis of hemoglobin. Fortunately there are many vegetable-based sources of iron, so meat is not our only source of iron. This is good news, because the hemoglobin that we get from eating red meat creates many problems in the body. When we eat red meat, the hemoglobin is broken down into globin, which is a protein molecule, and heme, an iron compound. Heme is thought to be the link between red meat and cancer. When heme is broken down, it forms dangerous chemicals called N-nitroso compounds. These compounds destroy the lining of the bowels, causing increased replication of the cells lining the bowel in order to heal the damaged bowel. The increased replication causes more errors in the cell's DNA, leading to cancer cell formation.

PROCESSED MEAT

Processed meat has been found to be more harmful than red meat. It is more strongly associated with bowel cancer than unprocessed red meat. One study showed that those who consumed processed meat had a 17 percent higher risk of developing bowel cancer than those who ate red unprocessed meat. Processed meat is meat that has been dried, smoked, salted, or canned. It includes biltong or beef jerky, sausages, boerewors, bacon, ham, corned beef, smoked meat, canned meat, and hot dogs. Eating processed meat regularly is associated with chronic diseases, like heart disease and cancer. These meat products contain sodium nitrite, which is used to preserve the red color of meat, prevent bacterial growth, and to add flavor. Sodium nitrate is converted to nitrosamines, which are cancer-causing compounds. Processed meat has been classified as a definite carcinogen (cancer-causing substance) and therefore is in the same group as smoking and alcohol intake. This means that eating processed meat is as dangerous as smoking and drinking alcohol.

BARBECUE, OR "BRAAI"

Burning meat with wood or charcoal leads to formation of harmful substances like polycyclic aromatic hydrocarbons (PAHs). These substances accumulate on the surface of meat that is barbecued or grilled on an open flame. PAHs have been shown to cause cancer. Heterocyclic compounds are other harmful chemical compounds that are formed when meat is barbecued or grilled on an open flame. Like PAPs, they have been shown to cause cancer.

SALT

Most of the time, meat is spiced by adding sodium chloride (salt) or salt-containing spices. Salt has been associated with an increase in blood pressure, strokes, and heart attacks. Food that is high in salt like barbecued (braai) meat has been shown to increase the risk of stomach cancer. Salt imposes many serious health risks that will be covered in detail in chapter 10.

FAST FOODS

Most people live on fast food, which has a high content of processed meats like burgers, bacon, sausages, etc. These unhealthy habits are also observed in the church, as evidenced by many Christians who suffer from diseases of lifestyle, like diabetes and hypertension. As discussed in the sections above, many cancers are diet-related. Fast foods contain a lot of salt, sugar, and fat, which result in high blood pressure, diabetes, and obesity. The complications of these conditions include heart attacks, heart failure, strokes, blindness, chronic obstructive lung diseases, gangrene, cancer, kidney failure, and premature aging. Sadly, most Christians are not even aware that they are hypertensive or diabetic, because these conditions are asymptomatic. Even those who are aware refuse to take treatment for religious reasons. They believe that they have enough faith, so they don't need medication. However the reality is that many Christians die from these conditions. At face value, it may seem that faith does not work. That is far from the truth. Faith works. Christ says if we have faith nothing will be impossible to us. He goes on to say we only need faith the size of a mustard seed to move mountains. Cleary the issue is not faith. Then why are people dying from diseases of lifestyle, if they have faith? The answer to this question is found in the book of James ("Faith without actions is dead" [Jas 2:17]). People have faith that God will heal them, but their faith is not accompanied by actions. To conquer diseases of lifestyle like high blood pressure and diabetes, faith must be accompanied by appropriate actions, by eating healthy. God does not honor faith that is not accompanied by obedience to his word. Scripture teaches us that we must take care of our bodies, because they are the temple of the Holy Spirit.

Chapter 6

Hunger Is the Best Cure

The saying that goes "Hunger is the best cook" should be rephrased as "Hunger is the best cure." There is mounting scientific evidence that attests to the health benefits of hunger. During the low caloric state of hunger, the body goes through a self-healing process. This is why fasting has been shown to be protective against cancer, autoimmune disease, diabetes, heart diseases, brain diseases, and kidney diseases. In a pilot study I conducted on forty people, of which twenty partook in the twenty-one-day Daniel Fast, and twenty did not fast, I compared cardiovascular parameters like arterial stiffness and intima media thickness (measure of plaque formation in the carotid artery) between the two groups. The two groups were matched by age and gender. The results showed significant differences between the groups. The people who fasted had lower arterial stiffness and intima media thickness compared to the non-fasting group. Increased arterial stiffness and increased intima media thickness are associated with cardiovascular outcomes like strokes and heart attacks. Even though the results of this study are not conclusive because it was a pilot study, they are in agreement with many other studies showing that fasting reduces the chances of strokes and heart attacks. In the next sections, we explore the physiological mechanisms that underlie the health benefits of fasting.

AUTOPHAGY

This term seems like a complex terminology, but all it means is "self-eating." It is derived from the Greek words "auto" and "phagy," which respectively mean "self" and "eating." During fasting, when nutrients are deficient, the body literally eats itself. This is the body's way of getting rid of old cell debris like membranes, mitochondria, proteins, etc. Once the old cell debris is ingested, its parts are reused to build new cell material. Autophagy is a very efficient recycling process that renews the body's machinery by bringing a balance between removal of old cell parts and formation of new ones. If autophagy is suppressed, new cell parts are not formed and damaged cell debris accumulates in the body. Consequently, the organs of the body do not function at their optimum level. The worst-case scenario is that damaged mitochondria may code for the synthesis of cancer cells. So, autophagy is a body's cleansing process that protects us by removing sub-standard cell parts that may predispose us to cancer.

FASTING PROMOTES BODY CLEANSING

Fasting is one of the main stimulants of autophagy. During fasting, insulin levels go down and glucagon secretion increases. The concentration of these hormones in our blood is controlled by food. When we eat, the levels of insulin increase and glucagon decreases, but when we fast, the levels of insulin decrease and glucagon increases. Increased concentration of glucagon during fasting is the stimulus for autophagy. This explains why people who fast regularly are healthier and have a longer lifespan than people who do not fast. It is a known fact that a car that is not serviced does not function properly and eventually breaks down because of the worn-out parts that are not replaced. Similarly, in people who do not fast, there is accumulation of worn-out cellular material that leads to sickness, premature aging, and neurodegeneration. This is due to accumulation of damaged proteins. It is for this reason that Christ makes it obligatory for his followers to fast.

FASTING IMPROVES BRAIN FUNCTION

When autophagy is reduced, brain neurons degenerate through a process known as neurodegeneration. The protein debris is toxic and is thought to be involved in the pathogenesis of neurodegenerative diseases like Parkinson's and Alzheimer's disease. Parkinson's disease is caused by reduced production of the hormone "dopamine" due to nerve cell breakdown. Nerve cells produce dopamine, which is required to control body movements. As the nerve cells degenerate, they do not secrete enough dopamine and the brain loses its ability to control movements. Consequently, the main symptom of Parkinson's is a tremor. Other symptoms include problems with movement, inability to balance, muscle stiffness, and slow movements. As the disease progresses, the person may have trouble swallowing and speaking. On the other hand, Alzheimer is a neurodegenerative type of dementia caused by brain cell death. The most common symptom of Alzheimer's is memory loss, especially in areas of learning and recalling new information. The person may also struggle to find the right words to use during a conversation. As the disease progresses, the person may undergo personality changes and engage in socially unacceptable behavior, like undressing in public. Fasting is protective against both Parkinson's and Alzheimer's disease. During fasting, toxic protein debris is removed from the brain through autophagy, resulting in reduced neurodegeneration and increased brain function.

Evidence of the beneficial effects of fasting on brain function is increasing. Research has shown that fasting for one or two days a week can protect the brain from degenerative brain diseases like Parkinson's and Alzheimer's. Reducing food intake by dieting is not beneficial; rather, completely stopping food intake for one or two days a week through fasting is the only beneficial method. During the period of fasting, damaged neuronal cell debris is digested by autophagosomes, and the products of digestion are used to synthesize new brain cells. An increase in neuronal cell growth results in improved brain function, demonstrated by improved memory. Thus, fasting makes learning easier, and the effects of Parkinson's and Alzheimer's are counteracted by the increased cell growth. All these important benefits of fasting bring us to the realization that the word of God is an important means to a life of abundance that Christ promises his followers.

FASTING SLOWS DOWN THE AGING PROCESS

Aging is a biological process that results from a number of factors. These biological factors contribute to a progressive decrease in cognitive and physical function. To date, fasting is the only non-genetic intervention that is known to reverse the effects of aging. A number of biological mechanisms involved in the increase in the lifespan of people who fast have been suggested. One of these mechanisms is thought to be "reduced oxidative stress." Oxygen radicals are the waste products of metabolic processes in the body. They are also produced when a person is under stress. They are very toxic and can destroy cells, cell membranes, DNA, enzymes, and proteins. This results in symptoms of aging like wrinkled skin, cancers, arthritis, osteoporosis, grey hair, balding, cataracts, and body stiffness. Fasting slows down the aging process by deregulating the expression of genes involved in oxidative stress. During fasting, oxygen radicals in the body are reduced. This reduces the oxidative damage of cells. Another mechanism is "increased mitochondrial respiratory efficiency." This means that during fasting the mitochondria function very efficiently using up oxygen to produce energy. This protects a number of organs from age-related decline in mitochondrial activity. That is why people who fast age slower and are more energetic than people who do not fast. All these effects result in a prolonged lifespan in people who practice fasting. Consequently, fasting has received a lot of attention from the scientific community. These benefits of fasting are observed in people who fast for two days a week. If benefits are observed in people who fast only two days a week, the benefits are even larger in a prolonged fasting like the twenty-one-day Daniel Fast.

FASTING PROTECTS THE BODY AGAINST CANCER

The processes of autophagy can suppress formation of cancer cells in the early stages of tumorigenesis (cancer cell formation). Fasting plays an important role in cancer prevention. In people who do not fast, autophagy may be deficient. This could lead to accumulation of deficient mitochondria and the subsequent increase in oxygen radicals. Oxygen radicals damage DNA, causing mutations that result in the formation of cancer cells. Fasting also promotes the recycling of damaged mitochondria. During the recycling process, mitochondria are digested and used for energy. If these damaged mitochondria are not recycled, they can lead to the synthesis of cancer cells.

Cancer cells grow very quickly—therefore, they have a very high metabolic demand. For survival, they need a lot of nutrients; hence, the low caloric state of fasting is not conducive for the growth of cancer cells. Fasting protects against cancer in three ways: it reduces oxygen radicals that damage DNA-causing mutation that code for cancer cells, promotes recycling of damaged mitochondria that lead to synthesis of cancer cells, and promotes a low caloric environment that is not conducive for the growth of cancer cells. It is important to clarify at this point that while fasting prevents cancer, there is no evidence that it cures cancer.

FASTING PREVENTS STROKES AND HEART ATTACKS

A free-flowing blood clot, also known as a thrombus, is very dangerous. These blood clots are formed inside blood vessels, and can travel to the brain and block one of the vessels that supply the brain with oxygen, resulting in a stroke, or it can travel to the heart and block one of the coronary arteries that supply the heart with oxygen, resulting in a heart attack. The smooth surface of blood vessels prevents formation of blood clots, but oxygen radicals can damage the smooth endothelial surface, resulting in intravascular blood clot formation. Fasting plays an important role in the prevention of intravascular blood clot formation because during fasting, fewer oxygen radicals are formed—therefore, the integrity of the vascular surface is maintained.

In a study I conducted in January of 2015 on a group of participants who were on the twenty-one-day Daniel Fast, I was able to show that after the fast, participants had reduced cholesterol, low density lipoproteins (LDL), and triglycerides. Cholesterol and triglycerides are known to mediate the formation of atherosclerotic plagues that may result in the formation of intravascular blood clots. Reduction of cholesterol and triglycerides means people who fast reduced their chance of a stroke or a heart attack. The participants in the January 2015 study also had reduced arterial stiffness. This means their blood vessels were less stiff compared to people who did not participate in the fast. Since stiff arteries have been shown to be an independent risk factor for strokes and heart attacks, people who fast have a reduced chance of suffering from strokes or heart attacks.

Chapter 7

Fruits and Vegetables Are God's Medicines

"Do you not know that your body is a temple of the Holy Spirit, who is in you, whom you have received from God? You are not your own; you were bought at a price. Therefore honor God with your body" (1 Cor 6:19–20). The focal point of this scripture in its original context is sexual sin however its meaning extends far beyond sexual immorality. Honoring God with our bodies includes ensuring that our bodies are healthy. A diet rich in fruits and vegetables is crucial for maintaining our bodies in peak physical condition, because these foods contain nutrients that are vital for the normal function of our body systems. They also play a very important role in protecting the body against different types of diseases, including diseases of lifestyle like type-2 diabetes and hypertension. Moreover, they are cheaper than drugs and do not have side effects. It is for this reason that fruits and vegetables have received a lot of attention from clinical researchers. Current research focuses on dietary intervention to prevent diseases like diabetes, hypertension, and cancer. Most of the foods that form part of the Daniel Fast, like fruits, vegetable, legumes, and nuts, have been shown to reduce the risk of cancer and other chronic diseases.

The most important thing that distinguishes the Daniel Fast from other fasts is what you eat and when you eat during the fast.

These two concepts are governed by age and health status. The first age group that can enter into the Daniel Fast are teenagers (ages thirteen to nineteen). This group enters into a special Daniel Fast. This type of fast, specific for teenagers, is explained in detail in chapter 11. If you are a teenager, you have to read chapter 11 carefully before you enter into the fast. The second group consists of young adults and adults (ages twenty to sixty-five). The final group consists of the elderly; i.e., those who are above sixty-five years. This group, like the teenage group, requires special attention. Chapter 12 focuses specially on this group. The age group that is left out are those below the age of thirteen. It is not recommended for this age group to partake in the fast because their young bodies cannot cope with the stresses imposed by the Daniel Fast.

WHEN TO EAT

Since hunger is an important part of the Daniel Fast for both physiological and spiritual benefits, it is recommended that the young adult and adult age group should only take meals from 6 p.m. to midnight. The main meal consisting of fruits and vegetables should be eaten as close to 6 p.m. as possible. This is to avoid eating a heavy meal late at night. The body's metabolic engine slows down at night and eating a heavy meal during that period may lead to weight gain. Ideally no heavy meal should be eaten after 9 p.m. This is to avoid overeating. After the main meal, only health snacks like unsalted nuts, dried fruits, popcorn, etc., may be eaten. Liquid intake during the entire fasting period is limited to water or caffeine-free tea. Water may be taken anytime during the day or night. Fruit juices are excluded because of their high sugar content. The time restrictions (eating only between 6 p.m. and midnight) apply to healthy adults (the twenty to sixty-five age group). This is to ensure that they get hungry and acquire the full benefits of autophagy, a concept that was explained in the previous chapter. The time restrictions do to not apply to the elderly, teenagers, or diabetics. The following section gives examples of some of the different foods that can be eaten and the nutrients they contain.

WHAT TO EAT

Proteins are the main building blocks of the body and they play an important role in cell growth and repair. Our muscles are made mainly of proteins. Animal products like meat, eggs, milk, cheese, etc., are rich in proteins, but they are not consumed during the Daniel Fast. This may lead to depletion of the body's protein stores, resulting in reduced muscle mass and, subsequently, muscle weakness. It is important to preserve muscle mass during the Daniel Fast by replacing meat and other animal products with non-animal based proteins. Good plant-based protein sources include beans, green peas, green beans, nuts such as almonds, peanut butter, soy beans, soy milk, lentils, and oats. These foods should be taken regularly during the fast to ensure that muscle mass is not lost.

Fruits

Oranges

Oranges are one of the most popular fruits in the world, renowned for their high concentration of vitamin C. Since they are rich in fiber and have a low glycemic index, they are a good snack for people with diabetes. Oranges are rich in nutrients, and some of those nutrients have healing properties. One of these nutrients, which has been shown to have a number of therapeutic properties, is "hesperidin." It is present almost exclusively in citrus fruits, like oranges and lemons. Numerous studies have shown that hesperidin protects the heart and blood vessels. It reduces blood pressure, and thus protects the heart and blood vessels from damage. It also lowers the amount of fats in the blood, resulting in reduced incidents of strokes and heart attacks in those people who eat oranges. As an antioxidant, hesperidin protects the blood vessels and other body organs against the damaging effects of oxidants, and it is well-established that antioxidants slow down the aging process. Besides hesperidin, oranges are also rich in vitamin C, which is a strong biological antioxidant.

Increased blood cholesterol is the major risk factor for heart attacks. High cholesterol causes formation of blood clots that block blood supply to the heart muscle, leading to its death. In experimental models, hesperidin was shown to decrease cholesterol by decreasing the absorption and synthesis of cholesterol. The protective effects of hesperidin are not only limited to the heart; it was also shown to reduce damage to the brain. Due to its antioxidant properties, it protects the brain from neurological disorders like Alzheimer's and Parkinson's disease. Due to the brain-protective properties of oranges, people who eat them have increased brain function, memory, ability to learn, concentration, and intelligence.

Bananas

Bananas are a rich source of vitamins, minerals, and fiber. They are known for their high content of potassium, which is important in the maintenance of normal blood pressure. Research has shown that people who consume foods high in potassium have a very low incidence of heart attacks. Due to their high glycemic index, diabetics must eat them with caution. Bananas also contain important compounds called "pectins," which are complex fibers that help in digestion. One of the pectins found in bananas is known as "fructooligosaccharide." This is a fructose-containing carbohydrate that is not digested by enzymes in our digestive tract. They play a very important role in increasing friendly bacteria, called *Bifidobacteria*, that regulate bowel function.

Grapes

Grapes are rich in phytonutrients that play an important role in longevity. Among these phytonutrients is "resveratrol," which is found in high concentrations in grape seed and grape skin. Eating whole grapes (including skin and seeds) is more beneficial than drinking grape juice. Resveratrol increases the expression of genes involved in longevity. The role of resveratrol in extending lifespan is similar to that of low calorie diet. Since the Daniel Fast diet is a low calorie diet, consumption of grapes during the fast results in longevity benefits from both the low calorie diet and resveratrol. Besides increasing lifespan, grapes have anticancer properties. They reduce the risk for breast, prostate, and colon cancer. The antioxidant activity of grapes is responsible for these properties. Seeds and skin have the highest concentration of antioxidants. Along with the longevity and anticancer properties, grapes have anti-inflammatory properties, which lower the risk of strokes and heart attacks.

Tomatoes

Tomatoes are a rich source of "lycopene," which has been identified as an antioxidant with anticancer properties. It has been found to reduce the risk of prostate cancer, which is one of the leading causes of death in aging men. A number of studies that have investigated the relationship between prostate cancer and lycopene have provided substantial evidence that lycopene reduces the risk of prostate cancer. Foods high in red meat, processed meat, white bread, and fried chips were associated with a high risk for prostate cancer. This signifies the importance that men partake in the fast because the Daniel Fast diet that consists of fruits and vegetables like tomatoes that are rich in lycopene.

Tomatoes have been shown to have health benefits due to their ability to lower cholesterol and triglycerides. They also prevent platelet aggregation (a crucial step in the formation of blood clots) thus preventing the formation of intravascular blood clots that can lead to strokes or heart attacks. Compared to other vegetables, they are rated as one of the most effective vegetables in the prevention of blood clot formation. This makes them important role players in the prevention of heart problems. Additionally, their protective role on the cardiovascular system is not limited to their ability to prevent blood clots; they also have powerful biological antioxidants like vitamin C, beta-carotene, and vitamin E. These antioxidants prevent the damage of blood vessels, thus improving cardiovascular health.

Pears

Pears are one of the most abundant nutrient-rich fruits. Together with apples, they have the highest source of "flavonoids." They reduce the concentration of secondary bile acids in the intestines, which are known to cause cancer. This makes them very important in the prevention of colon cancer. They are also very rich in fiber, and therefore play an important role in the prevention of constipation.

Strawberries

There is a lot of emerging evidence from research that strawberries provide several therapeutic benefits. Strawberries get their color from "anthocyanins," which are phenolic compounds. Consumption of anthocyanins reduces the risk of heart attacks by protecting the heart against coronary diseases. Strawberries are ranked among those fruits with the highest content of antioxidants. Other fruits in this category are cranberries, blackberries, and raspberries.

Plums/Prunes

Plums belong to the *Prunus* genus. When dried, they are called prunes. Both plums and prunes are rich in antioxidants, and therefore are effective in neutralizing dangerous antioxidants. They are also a good source of vitamin C, making them important in the absorption of iron. In addition to these benefits, prunes play an important role in bone metabolism. Research has shown that consumption of plums by post-menopausal women results in increased bone formation. Plums are rich in phenolic compounds like neo-chlorogenic acid and chlorogenic acid, which act as antioxidants, destroying free radicals, inhibiting bone resorption (removal of minerals like calcium from bones) and stimulating bone formation.

Peaches

Peaches (*Prunus persica*) have a variety of phenolic compounds which give them their antioxidant potency. Studies show that the peel of the peach contains a higher amount of phenolics and flavonols than the pulp. Additionally, peaches are rich in minerals like potassium, magnesium, calcium, manganese, and zinc, also found in high concentrations in the peel. This suggests that unpeeled peaches have more nutritional value than peeled peaches.

Apricots

Apricots are rich in vitamins, minerals, and beta-carotene. Their glycemic index can be rated as medium—therefore, people with diabetes must consume with caution, because they may raise blood sugar. Research has shown that they are protective against many cancers. Their anticancer properties may be due to the potent antioxidants found in apricots. Since they are rich in beta-carotene, they improve night vision.

Pineapple

Research has shown that consumption of pineapple results in increased serum melatonin concentration. "Melatonin" is an important antioxidant that may retard development of cancer and neurodegenerative diseases. Pineapples are also rich in vitamin C, which is an important biological antioxidant. Consumption of fruits that are rich in vitamin C, like pineapple, reduces the risk of age-related macular degeneration.

Mangos

Mangos contain numerous "phytochemicals" which have important nutritional value. They are also one of the richest sources of vitamin C, which among other things is very important for wound healing. They have a moderate concentration of "folate," which is required for the synthesis of red blood cells.

Avocados

Avocados have many health benefits because of the antioxidants and monounsaturated fatty acids they contain. Their health benefits include anti-inflammation, heart health, regulation of blood sugar, and anticancer properties. About 75 percent of the avocado's energy content is derived from fat, but about 70 percent of that fat is monounsaturated fat, which is good for the heart and blood vessels. Research has shown that consumption of avocados results in reduced LDL cholesterol (harmful cholesterol) and an increase in HDL cholesterol (good cholesterol).

Vegetables

Onions

Onions and garlic belong to the *Allium* family. The health benefits of onion are related to its anti-carcinogenic (protection against cancer), antiaggregatory (inhibition of blood clot formation), hypoglycemic (reduction of blood sugar) and hypolipidemic (reduction of fats in the blood) effects. Evidence from human trials show that the organosulfur compounds in onion are responsible for its anticancer properties.

Bioactive compounds in onions include "quercetin," which has the ability to lower blood lipids and cholesterol. Furthermore, onion prevents the formation of blood clots inside the blood vessels by inhibiting formation of thromboxane A. Thromboxane A is responsible for platelet aggregation (clumping together of platelets). By lowering cholesterol and inhibiting thromboxane A, onion consumption reduces the risk of intravascular blood clot formation, and thus prevents strokes and heart attacks. Chopping of onions causes onion tissue degradation, resulting in the formation of thiosulfinates, which have anti-inflammatory and anti-asthmatic effects. Cooked anions have a reduced ability to prevent blood clot formation—therefore, eating raw onions as part of a salad is recommended. For those who do not prefer raw onion, research has shown that boiling reduces the flavonoid content of onion significantly, while frying resulted in the lowest loss. If frying is preferred, monounsaturated oil, like olive oil, should be used because it remains stable at high temperatures. Polyunsaturated oils such as sunflower oil are not recommended, because they are unstable and may form peroxides at high temperatures.

Onions are one of the major dietary sources of antioxidants. Their ability to destroy oxygen radicals is due to two flavonoids they contain: quercetin and "kaempferol." Besides its lipid-lowering effects, quercetin plays an important role in eliminating oxygen radicals. Kaempferol is a powerful antioxidant due to its ability to scavenge a number of oxygen radicals, including the superoxide anion. This reduction of oxygen radicals make kaempferol very important in cancer prevention. Oxygen radicals oxidize DNA, proteins, and lipids; this process results in cancer, heart diseases, neurodegenerative diseases, and inflammation. By destroying oxygen radicals, onions reduce the risk of developing these diseases. Some studies found that the carotenoids in spring onions protect against age-related eye diseases, including macular degeneration and cataracts. A high intake of onions is encouraged during the Daniel Fast.

Cabbage

Cabbage is closely related to broccoli, cauliflower, and brussels sprout. Collectively, these are known as cruciferous vegetables. These vegetables have similar health benefits. Cabbage has many benefits, including the lowering of blood cholesterol. It is an excellent source of vitamin C and vitamin K. It has important phytochemicals like sulforaphane and glucosinolates, which stimulate the production of detoxifying enzymes. These compounds are responsible for the cabbage's anticancer properties. Most of the beneficial properties of cabbage are lost when it is overcooked. Raw cabbage, or cabbage that is steamed for a short period, has the most benefits.

Broccoli

Broccoli, like other cruciferous vegetables, has received a lot of attention because of its anticancer properties. A phytochemical called "indole-3-carbinol" is responsible for these properties. Eating increased amounts of broccoli daily may cause regression of tumors or reduce their growth rate. Indole-3-carbinol is more effective in oestrogen-related cancers, like cervical and breast cancer. Other studies have shown that consumption of broccoli is protective against prostate cancer. Indole-3-carbinol is converted to diindolylmethane (DIM) in the stomach, and has the same anticancer properties. When broccoli is overcooked to the point where it becomes soft and mushy, it loses its nutritional value. Like cabbage, it must be steamed for a short duration for it to retain its nutritional value.

Cauliflower

Cauliflower has similar health benefits to broccoli, because both vegetables are rich in glucosinolates. Both vegetables also have the same ability against prostate cancer. Cauliflower is more effective in reducing the risk of colorectal cancer compared to broccoli. The nutritional value of cauliflower is the same whether cooked or uncooked, but boiling with water or overcooking reduces its nutritional value. To get the full nutritional value of broccoli, it must be consumed raw or steamed.

Spinach

There is a lot of evidence that diets rich in green leafy vegetables like spinach are protective against common chronic diseases, like cancer, obesity, diabetes, and high blood pressure. Spinach, which falls into this group, has a diverse nutritional composition, such as vitamins, minerals, and phytochemicals. It is also rich in vitamin E, which is a powerful antioxidant that protects blood vessels from damage, so it plays an important role in cardiovascular health. It also has a lot of fiber, and therefore plays an important role in digestion and the prevention of constipation. Spinach is a rich source of "carotenoids," which play an important role in the prevention of age-related cataracts. It contains more phenols than cabbage and lettuce. These phenols have antibacterial, antiviral, and antifungal properties (they protect us against bacteria, viruses, and fungal infections). Spinach and broccoli have the highest amounts of phenols compared to other vegetables—therefore, they have the highest antioxidant capacity. To get the full benefits of the Daniel Fast, these two vegetables—especially broccoli—must be consumed daily. Research has shown that consuming spinach daily for a period of twenty-one days, just like the Daniel Fast, results in increased antioxidants and reduced DNA damage. These studies highlight the importance of the Daniel Fast by providing concrete scientific evidence that the body's ability to fight cancer is increased during the Daniel Fast. Since cancer is one of the leading causes of death worldwide, the benefits of spinach consumption have received a lot of attention on the research front. Epidemiological studies have demonstrated that spinach is protective against many cancers like breast, colon, and esophageal cancer.

Potatoes

Potatoes are associated with obesity because of the way they are cooked. They are usually eaten as deep-fried, fat-filled French fries or potato chips. When they are properly prepared, they provide a lot of health benefits. They have antioxidant, hypocholesterolemic, anti-inflammatory, and anticancer effects. Studies on the role of potatoes in diabetes or weight management are inconclusive. Some studies support a positive effect, while other studies show a negative one. A cautious approach of minimizing potato intake is best for diabetic, as well as people who are overweight or obese. Besides the contradictory evidence on the detrimental effects of potatoes on diabetics and overweight people, potatoes offer a lot of health benefits to non-diabetics and people of normal weight. They contain a number of antioxidants that are protective against many age-related inflammatory diseases like arthritis, cancers, heart diseases, and neurodegenerative disorders. Potatoes are also rich in vitamin B6, which has many health benefits, including taking part in enzymatic reactions required for the synthesis of amino acids and DNA. Vitamin B6 is also necessary for normal brain function, because it is required for the synthesis of "amines," which are important neurotransmitters in the brain.

Carrots

Carrots are rich in beta-carotene, a precursor of vitamin A, which is a powerful antioxidant. It is also known to promote good night vision, as previously stated. Research has shown that people who consume carrots regularly have a significantly lower risk of developing cardiovascular health problems compared to people who do not eat carrots regularly. It is recommended that carrots should form part of our daily diet. Carrots produce compounds called "polyacetylenes," that are considered to contribute significantly to the health benefits associated with the consumption of carrots. They have a wide range of bioactivity, including anti-allergic, antibacterial, antifungal, anti-inflammatory, and anticancer activities. They inhibit the proliferation and growth of cancer cells. A carrot extract called "dichloromethane" was found to stimulate insulin-dependent glucose uptake by cells. This means carrots have anti-diabetic properties, and that they have the ability to lower blood glucose in diabetics and should form part of their version of the Daniel Fast diet.

Beets

Beets belong to the same family as spinach. Both the leaves and roots can be consumed. The leaves have most of the benefits of green leafy vegetables like spinach. The root, which is usually purple, can be cooked or eaten raw. Beets are rich in antioxidants, which have been shown to have important anti-inflammatory properties. The antioxidants in beets also prevent premature aging. To preserve nutritional quality, beets should not be cut before cooking but must be boiled whole. They can be diced after cooking.

Grains

Brown rice

Brown rice is a good replacement for processed staple foods like white rice, pasta, and maize porridge. When white rice is produced from brown rice, the milling and polishing removes all of the dietary fiber, most of the vitamins like vitamin B1, vitamin B3, vitamin B6, and important minerals like iron, phosphorus, and manganese. Besides these nutrients, brown rice is a rich source of copper and "selenium." Since both selenium and fiber have anticancer properties, brown rice is very important in the prevention of cancer. The anticancer properties of rice have been well established. Fiber increases the rate of gastrointestinal motility, thus minimizing the damage that can be caused by carcinogenic (cancer causing) substances. On the other hand, selenium prevents cancer through a process called "apoptosis." Apoptosis is programmed cell death, which is necessary for the normal growth and health of the body. In a normal human being, billions of cells fragment and die each day. This allows elimination of worn-out cells, and prevents proliferation of cancer cells. Besides preventing cancer through apoptosis, selenium has other anticancer properties because it is part of the active site of an enzyme called "glutathione peroxidase," which is a powerful antioxidant. Due to its content of selenium, brown rice is very important in the prevention of cancer and cardiovascular outcomes like strokes and heart attacks.

Sorghum

For people who cannot afford brown rice, sorghum (mabele), which is native to Africa, is a good alternative to brown rice because it is cheaper and it contains most of the nutrients found in brown rice like the vitamin B complex and magnesium. It is important in the prevention of certain cancers and diabetes. Its high fiber content makes it very important for the health of the digestive system. A serving of one cup (one hundred ninety-two grams) contains about 48 percent of the recommended daily fiber intake; therefore, it promotes gastrointestinal motility which prevents constipation and bowel cancer. Moreover, sorghum lowers blood cholesterol by preventing its absorption from the intestines. Consequently, people who include sorghum in their diet have a lower incidence of strokes and heart attacks. Besides lowering blood cholesterol, magnesium promotes cardiovascular health by lowering blood pressure. Like brown rice, sorghum is rich in magnesium, which is essential for the maintenance of normal blood pressure.

Herbs and Spices

Garlic

Garlic is a member of the *Allium* family and has many health benefits. It is known for its numerous therapeutic properties due to its sulphur-containing compound. The sulphur compounds are responsible for its antihypertensive, antidiabetic, and anti-obesity properties. The heating of garlic during cooking causes denaturation of the sulphur compounds, resulting in reduced anticancer and antibacterial potential. In order to get the full nutritional benefits of garlic, it must be consumed raw. It has many health benefits, including lowering blood pressure. Its antihypertensive (blood-pressure lowering) properties will be discussed in detail in chapter 10. In this section, we will focus on its antibacterial and anticancer properties.

ANTI-BACTERIAL PROPERTIES

Garlic has been used for centuries for its antibacterial properties. Besides killing bacteria, it has also been shown to be effective at killing viruses and parasites as well. Due to these properties, it has been used in the treatment of bacterial, viral, and parasitic infections. Most importantly, garlic was found to be effective in treating infections that have become resistant to antibiotic treatment. Antibiotic resistance has become a serious problem because of the overprescription of antibiotics. By treating these untreatable conditions, garlic has become very important in the control of infections.

Anticancer properties

Changing dietary habits has been shown to be a cost-effective way to prevent cancer. *Allium* vegetables like garlic and onion have also been associated with a reduced risk of certain cancers. Regular intake of garlic has been shown to lower the risk of most types of cancer. Garlic's anticancer properties depend on its ability to promote cell apoptosis (programmed cell death). When a cell is damaged and cannot function properly, it starts to dismantle itself and its parts are recycled. This is a very important process, because damaged cells can become cancerous. By promoting apoptosis, garlic protects the body against cancer. Garlic was also found to be protective against cancers caused by barbecuing (braai) or cooking meat at very high temperatures. When meat is cooked in a barbecue, nitrosamines and heterocyclic compounds are formed. Research has shown that these compounds are carcinogenic (they cause cancer). Daily consumption of garlic is effective in inhibiting the format of the carcinogenic nitrosamines. Garlic has been found to be protective against the cancers listed below:

Esophageal cancer

This is cancer of the esophagus. Consumption of raw garlic once a week was found to be protective against esophageal cancer. Increasing this rate of consumption resulted in an increased protective value.

Stomach cancer

Case-controlled studies have shown that consumption of large quantities of garlic decreases the risk of stomach cancer.

Colorectal cancer

This is cancer of the colon (large intestine) and rectum. Research evidence shows that garlic consumption reduces the risk of this cancer.

Prostate cancer

This type of cancer is more prevalent in older men. It develops very slowly over a period of years without any visible symptoms. That is why men over the age of forty years are advised to do a prostate cancer test at least once a year. Consumption of garlic is protective against prostate cancer.

Other cancers

High intake of garlic is associated with a reduced risk of the following cancers: endometrial cancer, ovarian cancer, cancer of the oral cavity, pharyngeal cancer and laryngeal cancer.

Ginger

Ginger is good for relaxing and calming the intestinal tract by eliminating intestinal gas. Due to its ability to eliminate gastrointestinal distress, it is very effective in preventing symptoms of motion sickness like nausea, vomiting, and dizziness. It also has antioxidant and anti-inflammatory properties. Its anti-inflammatory effects are due to compounds called "gingerols," which are effective in relieving pain for patients with osteoarthritis and rheumatoid arthritis. Not only does ginger relieve pain, but it also reduces swelling and improves movement. The anti-inflammatory effects of ginger are due to its ability to suppress pro-inflammatory cytokines produced in the joints.

Like garlic, ginger has anticancer properties. Experiments have shown that the phytonutrients in ginger induce apoptosis in ovarian cancer cells, resulting in the death of the cancer cells. Ovarian cancer is very dangerous, because it is asymptomatic until the cancer is at an advanced stage. Consumption of ginger is therefore very important in the prevention of ovarian cancer. Moreover, cancer cells do not develop resistance to ginger, even after prolonged exposure. This makes ginger very important in fighting ovarian cancer because ovarian cancer cells have been shown to develop resistance to drugs that are used to treat ovarian cancer.

Turmeric

Turmeric contains a substance with a yellow pigment called "curcumin." Other bioactive components include: demethoxycurcumin, bis-demethoxycurcumin, and turmeric essential oils which are responsible for turmeric's therapeutic properties. These compounds have been found effective in the treatment of arthritis (a joint disorder characterized by inflammation of the joints, which may result in pain). The most common form of arthritis is osteoarthritis. Anti-inflammatory drugs are used to treat arthritis, but long-term use results in inadequate pain relief, ulcers, and cardiovascular problems. It is for this reason that research is now focusing on herbal remedies for the relief of inflammation. Turmeric is one natural remedy that is effective in the treatment of arthritis. Additionally, a number of animal studies have shown that turmeric is effective in the prevention of cancer. This implies that regular consumption of turmeric may be protective against cancer.

Cayenne pepper, chili pepper, red pepper, and green pepper

All these are fruits of the plant genus *Capsicum* (peppers). They contain a number of compounds that are responsible for the fruit's therapeutic properties. The spicy ones, like the cayenne pepper and the chili pepper, are called "chillies." Their therapeutic properties include prevention of blood clot formation inside the blood vessels and prevention of atherosclerosis. Both of these properties reduce the chances of a stroke or heart attack. Capsicum also aids bowel movement by stimulating peristalsis. Some studies have shown that capsicum has anticancer properties.

Research on the benefits of vegetables is ongoing. What is known now may be just a tip of the iceberg. As more knowledge becomes available, vegetables may even surpass medication in the prevention and control of chronic medical conditions like diabetes.

Chapter 8

The Daniel Fast for People who Are Overweight or Obese

WHEN IT COMES TO overeating and obesity, a harsh statement from the book of Proverbs gives us a very rude awakening, "Put a knife to your throat if you are given to gluttony" (Prov 23:2). According to this verse, it is clear that overeating is equated to suicide. In the Christian framework, suicide is frowned upon, but gluttony is accepted. The effects of overeating may not be as acute as those of suicide, but it is essentially the same thing. When you overeat, you are killing yourself slowly, and there is a lot of scientific evidence to prove this. Obesity is on the rise worldwide in spite of the many dietary advices and over-the-counter quick-fixes. Instead of solving the problem, these quick-fixes and diet programs seem to have exacerbated it. Many diet fads have come and gone over the centuries, but none of them have helped in the alleviation of the obesity epidemic. The problem with these diets is that they promote consumption or rejection of one food type. For example, complete elimination of fat was proposed as the best way to lose weight; however, this did not work because certain types of fats, like Omega-3, are essential for cardiovascular health. Then, rich protein diets were advocated as the best way to lose weight. Sadly, these have serious side effects, related to kidney problems. Lately, in countries like South Africa, the low carb Banting Diet has a cult following. Though this diet may provide short-term benefits to diabetics, its long-term side effects may be detrimental, as carbohydrates play an important role in the body. On the other hand, the Daniel Fast is a balanced, short-term, low-calorie eating plan that detoxes the body. Elimination of processed sugar and other processed foods like bread and cakes makes it ideal for weight loss.

WHAT IS OBESITY?

Let us take a moment to define obesity. Obesity is a medical condition in which there is accumulation of excess body fat. People with a body mass index (BMI) between twenty-five and thirty kg/m^2 are overweight, and those with a BMI of thirty and above are considered obese. People who are obese are predisposed to heart disease, high blood pressure, type 2 diabetes, chronic obstructive pulmonary disease (COPD), sleep apnea, and cancer. To avoid these diseases, a BMI below twenty-five kg/m^2 must be targeted. For some it may not be possible to reach a BMI below twenty-five within the twenty-one-day period, but if they maintain the good diet of the Daniel Fast beyond the twenty-one days and continue avoiding foods that are high in processed carbohydrates, they may reach their target weight.

Obesity results from a combination of factors like excessive food intake, lack of exercise, endocrine disorders, and genetic disorders. Excess food intake and lack of exercise are the major causes of obesity. Surprisingly, excess carbohydrate consumption is more associated with obesity than excess fat consumption. Sweetened soft drinks, cakes, pap (a traditional African dish in some countries), pasta, chips, white bread, dumpling, etc., contribute significantly to the rising incident of obesity. Lack of exercise also plays a significant role in obesity. Urbanization and improved technology means that fewer people do manual labour. Added to this is the improvement of the public transport system, especially the rise of the taxi industry, which has resulted in fewer people walking to work or to train stations. Children spend hours in front of television screens, or computer screens playing games. This has resulted in an increase of childhood obesity. From the current evidence, it is clear that lack of exercise and increased food intake are the two main reasons for the increasing incident of obesity. Fortunately, both of them are modifiable factors.

Even in people who are genetically predisposed to obesity, i.e., those with increased fat mass due to their genetic makeup, they do not progress from normal weight to obesity without excess food intake. Just like genetics, a sedentary lifestyle (lack of exercise) cannot lead to obesity in the absence of excess food intake. This leads to a conclusion that excess food intake is central to the development of obesity. Many food guidelines have been developed over the years, but they do not seem to work. The number of overweight and obese people is increasing worldwide, due to poor dietary choices. Epidemiological studies have provided evidence that consumption of fruits and vegetables leads to weight loss, because these nutrients have carbohydrates of a low energy density. Consequently, diseases that are associated with obesity (i.e., Type 2 diabetes, cardiovascular problems, and cancer) can be avoided. This brings to light the importance of the twenty-one-day Daniel Fast. The likelihood that the Daniel Fast will succeed, if conducted properly, where weight-loss diets and dietary guidelines have failed, is due to its holistic approach to the problem of obesity. Unlike other interventions, which only take a one-dimensional approach, the Daniel Fast takes a three-dimensional approach by addressing the triune nature of the human being: body, spirit, and soul.

REDUCED FOOD INTAKE IS BENEFICIAL FOR OVERWEIGHT OR OBESE PEOPLE

People who are overweight or obese and who do not have diabetes, should follow the strict "one-meal-a-day" diet plan during the Daniel Fast. Calorie restriction and food with a low calorie density are two essential elements that should be part of the weight-loss plan for people who are obese. A meal consisting of fruits and vegetables should be taken at 6 p.m. daily and no food should be taken after 10 p.m. Studies have shown that eating late at night leads to weight gain. Fruit juices should be avoided because of their high sugar content. Recommended drinks are water, rooibos tea, and green tea (without any added sugar). Research has shown that sugar contributes significantly to obesity.

IMPORTANT WEIGHT REDUCTION FOODS

Spinach

Spinach is one vegetable that is essential for people who intend to lose weight during the Daniel Fast, because it has been found to have anti-obesity properties. It is full of nutrients, but very low in calories, and that makes it perfect for people who wish to lose weight. Some of the nutrients found in spinach are "thylakoids," which induce satiety by slowing down the digestion and absorption of dietary fats. This increases the content of fat in the small intestines, and the increased fat content diminishes the feeling of hunger. Thylakoids from spinach have another effect in the body: they stimulate the release of a hormone called "cholecystokinin" (CCK) which lessens the feeling of hunger. Two other hormones are stimulated after spinach consumption, glucagon-like peptide-1 (GLP-1), and leptin. These two hormones also promote satiety. High levels of these satiety hormones in circulation lead to a significant reduction of appetite.

Garlic

Garlic is well-known for its antihypertensive, anti-inflammatory, and anticancer properties but little is known about its anti-obesity effects. A sulphur compound in garlic known as "thiacremonone" is responsible for its anti-obesity effects. The anti-obesity effects of garlic are still at an early stage of research. What is known from recent research is that garlic regulates the number of fat cells formed in the body through its anti-inflammatory properties. Research has shown that pre-adipocytes mature into fully fledged adipocytes (fat cells) under certain inflammatory conditions. The sulphur compounds in garlic inhibit inflammation, thus preventing the conversion of pre-adipocytes into matured adipocytes.

Peanuts

There is a general belief that peanuts cause weight gain; however, research has shown the opposite. People who eat peanuts at least twice a week are less likely to gain weight compared to people who do not consume peanuts. The effect of peanuts on weight may be due to the action of trypsin inhibitors. Peanut consumption significantly reduces weight gain, food intake, and fasting glucose levels. They also increase the feeling of satiety, leading to reduced food intake. Snacking on peanuts during the Daniel Fast can be beneficial to overweight or obese people.

Chili Pepper (Chillies)

Chillies are rich in "capsaicinoids" which also have valuable anticancer, anti-inflammatory, and antioxidant properties. Research has also shown that they are beneficial to overweight and obese people because of the role they play in weight reduction. Weight is reduced through three processes: increased energy expenditure, increased breakdown of fats, and reduced appetite.

Increased energy expenditure

Increasing metabolic rate is one of the most effective methods of weight reductions. Most of the drugs used to increase metabolic rate have undesirable side effects—therefore, they are not recommended for long term use. Chili peppers have no known severe side effect because they can form part of normal diet. It is for this reason that their ability to increase energy expenditure in the body has stirred a lot of interest.

Increased fat breakdown

There is mounting evidence that chili peppers increase the breakdown of fats, especially in people with a high BMI. Most importantly, it is effective in reducing fat that is stored around the abdominal area. Central obesity (increased fat around the abdomen) is associated with cardiovascular events like strokes and heart attacks. This effect of chili peppers on central obesity could be very beneficial to men in particular, because they store most of their fat around the waist. Chili peppers reduce fat by inhibiting the maturation of pre-adipocytes (immature fat cells) to adipocytes (matured fat cells). The ultimate result is the reduction in the number and size of fat cells.

Suppression of appetite

Consumption of chili peppers results in the increased feeling of satiety. The mechanism of how chili peppers suppress appetite is not well understood, but it is speculated that chili peppers increase the secretion of certain gut hormones, which decrease appetite.

It is important for overweight or obese people to adopt a healthy eating lifestyle, even when the fast is over. If healthy eating habits are combined with the spiritual disciplines of the fast, overweight people can enjoy the benefits of living a normal weight and a healthy lifestyle.

Chapter 9

The Daniel Fast for People with Diabetes

WHAT IS DIABETES?

Diabetes mellitus, commonly known as diabetes, is a disease in which there is high blood sugar over a long period. In those who do not have the disease, after eating a meal containing sugar, blood sugar increases, but then it is taken into the cells and it drops back to normal. In people with diabetes, the blood sugar does not return to normal, but remains high for a long period. Diabetes is a serious disease that can lead to strokes, blindness, kidney failure, and foot ulcers. There are two main types of diabetes, Type 1 and Type 2. In Type 1 diabetes, the pancreas fails to produce insulin (a hormone that is required to transport glucose from the blood to the cells). Type 2 diabetes is caused by insulin resistance. The most common cause of Type 2 diabetes is increased body weight.

CAN DIABETICS PARTICIPATE IN THE DANIEL FAST?

A healthy diet is one of the best ways to control diabetes. It can even go as far as preventing diabetes in overweight and obese people. The Daniel Fast diet, consisting of fruits and vegetables, is the best diet for people with diabetes. Research has shown that a vegetarian diet is clinically beneficial in the management of diabetes. Fruits and vegetables are very high in fiber, which slows the absorption of sugar from the intestines, thus lowering blood sugar. In addition to controlling blood sugar, the fruit and vegetable diet offers health benefits for the heart. It is protective against strokes and heart attacks because it reduces fats in the blood (LDL cholesterol) and lowers blood pressure. Weight loss is another benefit of the Daniel Fast. Due to low calorie intake there is loss of visceral fat. Visceral fat (fat in the abdomen) is very unhealthy, and is associated with many cardiovascular problems (problems related to the heart and blood vessels) such as strokes and heart attacks. Visceral fat is also implicated in diabetes. Therefore, the fruit and vegetable diet solves both blood sugar problems and heart problems.

It is important to emphasize that during the Daniel Fast, the eating pattern for people with diabetes should be different from the pattern of healthy people. For normal healthy people, the recommendation is that they should only eat one meal a day in the evening at 6 p.m. Since people with diabetes cannot go for prolonged periods without food, as their blood sugar may drop dangerously, they are allowed to eat during the day. Their diet, however, should still be confined to fruits and vegetables.

The Daniel Fast diet is a low glycemic index diet, so it may lower blood sugar levels back to normal. Even though blood sugar may return to normal, people are encouraged to continue taking their medication, unless a doctor advises them to reduce the dose. Contrary to what other Christians believe, taking medication is not an indication of little faith. It is important to remember that the wisdom that the doctors have is from God, and that the core element of the Daniel Fast is prayer. Medication is not taken as a final solution, but prayer for complete healing from diabetes should continue during the fast. With God, nothing is impossible. A time will come when healing will completely manifest, and medication will not be required.

WHAT TO EAT

People with diabetes must eat foods with a low glycemic index. The glycemic index measures the effect of food on blood sugar. Foods that increase blood sugar rapidly have a high glycemic index. An example is glucose, which has a glycemic index of one hundred. Most fruits and vegetables have a low glycemic index, and therefore are safe for consumption. Not all fruits and vegetables have a low glycemic level. For example, potatoes have a medium-to-high glycemic index. Even though fruits are sweet, they are safe for people with diabetes, because the sugar in fruits, fructose, has a low glycemic index.

MAGNESIUM AND THE CONTROL OF BLOOD SUGAR

The role of magnesium in diabetes has been ignored by most doctors because the results of clinical studies are still limited, but there is mounting evidence that magnesium plays an important role in the control of blood pressure. Several studies have indicated that magnesium helps regulate blood glucose by improving insulin sensitivity. Consumption of foods that are rich in magnesium like whole grains, green leafy vegetables, beans and nuts during the Daniel Fast could help control the blood pressure of those who are diabetic, and reduce the risk of type-2 diabetes for those who are not diabetic. What makes magnesium so important in glucose homeostasis is that it is a cofactor for many enzymes involved in glucose metabolism. The following food groups are considered to be rich in magnesium:

- Green leafy vegetables: spinach, broccoli, cabbage, and turnip greens
- Whole grains: brown rice, sorghum (or mabele), barley, and oats.
- Beans and lentils: kidney beans, white beans, and black-eyed peas.
- Nuts and seeds: almonds, peanuts, cashews, and pumpkin seeds.

OTHER FOODS THAT SHOULD BE PART OF THE DIET PLAN FOR DIABETICS

Apples

Diabetes mellitus is a serious disorder with many complications. The prevalence of this condition is increasing worldwide, and is imposing a serious financial burden in developing countries with limited resources. This has led researchers to focus on natural remedies that are less expensive and have fewer or no side effects. Apples, with their phytochemicals, have the ability to lower blood sugar and have become a focus of research. They are a good snack for people with diabetes, because they contain a number polyphenolic compounds which are effective in the control of many chronic diseases, including diabetes. Some therapeutic compounds are found in the apple peel—therefore, it is important to eat the peel with the apple. Besides their antidiabetic properties, apples have beneficial effects against aging, cancer, cardiovascular diseases, bone diseases, lung diseases, and Alzheimer's disease.

Diabetes mellitus is also known to result in hyperlipidemia (an increased concentration of fats in the blood). This is a major risk for strokes and heart attacks. These fats are increased in diabetics, because the body cannot use glucose for energy, due to insulin resistance. This results in the mobilization of fats from the adipose tissue resulting in increased concentration of fats in the blood. Experimental data suggests that consumption of apples for twenty-one days leads to a significant reduction in the concentration of fats in the blood. These experiments prove without a doubt that the polyphenolic components of apples have lipid-lowering effects. This implies that diabetics can benefit significantly if they consume at least one apple a day over the twenty-one-day Daniel Fast period.

Garlic

The health benefits of garlic have been known for centuries, as many communities in different parts of the world have used it medicinally as a spice. The sulphur compound that was discussed in the previous chapter, in relation to its anti-obesity properties, was found to be also responsible for its anti-diabetic properties. Experiments revealed that garlic increases adipose tissue sensitivity to insulin, resulting in increased glucose uptake by the cells and the subsequent reduction of blood glucose. This means that people with diabetes can substantially benefit by using garlic to spice their vegetables during the Daniel Fast. It is important to emphasize that garlic should not be used as a replacement for prescribed medication.

Onion

Research has shown that onion has hypoglycemic (ability to lower blood sugar) effects. It also reduces the chances of diabetic nephropathy, due to its cholesterol-lowering effects. Renal lesions that result from diabetes are reduced by onion. These research findings suggest that adding onions while cooking is beneficial for diabetics.

Pears

Pears have a high fiber content, both of soluble and insoluble fiber. Intake of dietary fiber has been shown to reduce the risk of type 2 diabetes. Besides the fiber, pears have important flavonols that increase insulin sensitivity. Regular consumption of pears provides adequate supply of these flavonols, resulting in reduced blood glucose due to increased insulin sensitivity.

Strawberries

Strawberries have a low glycemic index—therefore, they are a suitable snack for diabetics during the Daniel Fast. In addition to their low glycemic index, they regulate blood sugar. In both animal and human experiments, strawberries ware associated with a significant reduction in blood sugar. In a recent discovery, scientists found that people who had high blood sugar because of increased sugar intake (a sugar spike) could reduce their blood sugar level by eating strawberries. Another mechanism thought to be responsible for the strawberries' ability to regulate blood sugar is the inhibition of carbohydrate digestive enzymes. This makes consumption of strawberries during the Daniel Fast vital very important in people with type 2 diabetes as they help in the maintenance of normal blood sugar levels.

GLYCEMIC INDEX (GI)

Diabetics must be aware of the glycemic index (GI) of the food they consume. GI gives important information on how fruits or vegetables increase blood sugar. Fruits and vegetables that have a lower GI are more appropriate for diabetics.

Glycemic Index Scores

Low GI: 55 and below, very good for diabetics.

Moderate GI: 56 to 69, should be consumed in moderation by diabetics.

High GI: 70 and above, should be avoided or taken in very small servings.

Classification of fruits and vegetables according to their Glycemic Index

Low Glycemic Index

Cherries	22
Grapefruit	25
Prunes	29
Apricot	31
Oranges	33
Apples	38
Pears	38
Plum	38
Strawberries	40
Peaches	41
Mango	51
Kiwi fruit	53

Moderate Glycemic Index

Grapes	59
Pawpaw	59
Figs	61
Sweet potato	61
Raisins	64
Beets	64

High Glycemic Index

Bananas	70
Watermelon	72
Maize meal porridge	74
Pumpkin	75
Potato	85
White rice	85

The above list is not exhaustive, but it gives an example of the most common fruits and vegetables that are consumed around the world. Diabetics are advised to find the glycemic index of fruits and vegetables that are not listed above. Most importantly, diabetics are advised to plan their Daniel Fast with the help of a health care professional.

EXAMPLE OF A DIABETIC MEAL PLAN

People with diabetes should not skip meals. They must eat three meals a day to ensure that the blood sugar levels do not drop to dangerous levels. However they must still maintain the strict fruit-and-vegetable Daniel Fast diet. An example of a three-meal diet is given below:

Breakfast

The following meals are recommended for breakfast:

- Oats, Weet-Bix, or sorghum (mabele) soft porridge with soy milk
- One fruit

Lunch

Lunch should not be a heavy meal. The following is recommended:

- One bowl of lentils or bean soup
- One fruit

Supper

Supper is the main meal of the day. It should be taken at 6 p.m.

- Brown rice or sorghum (mabele) as a staple
- Tomato gravy with herbs and spices (use tomatoes, onion, garlic, ginger, and turmeric)
- One fruit

People with diabetes can benefit a lot from the Daniel Fast. It is very important that that they do not skip meals to avoid a dangerous drop in glucose. Fruits must be carefully selected from the low GI group of fruits. A proper diet and prayer is the best therapy for diabetes.

Chapter 10

The Daniel Fast for People with Hypertension

WHAT IS HYPERTENSION?

BLOOD PRESSURE IS MEASURED using two values: systolic and diastolic blood pressure. Blood pressure is normal if systolic blood pressure is less than one hundred forty mm Hg (millimeters of mercury), and if diastolic blood pressure is less than ninety mm Hg. People with a blood pressure above these values are said to be hypertensive. This condition of increased blood pressure is dangerous if it is not treated. The increased pressure inside the blood vessels can destroy the endothelial layer (a thin layer of cells that form the lining of the inner surface of blood vessels) of the blood vessels, leading to formation of atherosclerotic plaques (build-up of fatty substances on the inner surface of the blood vessels). These plaques can lead to narrowing and hardening of the blood vessels. Under these conditions it is easy for intravascular blood clots to form, which can lead to strokes or heart attacks. High blood pressure can also destroy the body's vital organs like the brain, kidneys, and heart. Sadly, high blood pressure is asymptomatic (people who have this condition do not display any visible or traceable symptoms). They can live with undetected hypertension for years while it is destroying target organs. That is why it is known as the silent killer. In spite of all the research that has been conducted on hypertension, it is still the leading cause of death in the world. The church is not immune to the scourge of hypertension. Many Christians are hypertensive, and many die from complications related to hypertension. Unfortunately, even those who are aware of their hypertensive status refuse to take treatment, because they believe their faith will protect them. The reality is that we bury a lot of Christians who die from strokes, heart attacks, and kidney failure caused by high blood pressure. At face value, it may seem that faith does not work against hypertension; however, that is far from the truth. Faith works. Christ says if we have faith, nothing will be impossible to us. He goes on to say we only need faith the size of a mustard seed to move mountains. Clearly, the issue is not faith. Why are people dying from the consequences of hypertension if they have faith? The answer to this question, as previously mentioned, is found in the book of James: "Faith without actions is dead"(Jas 2:17). Though people have faith that God will heal them, their faith is not accompanied by actions. To conquer diseases of lifestyle, like high blood pressure and diabetes, faith must be accompanied by appropriate actions, such as eating healthy. God does not honor faith that is not accompanied by obedience to his word. Scripture teaches us that we must take care of our bodies, because they are the temple of the Holy Spirit. Prayer for healing must be followed by healthy living. One of the methods of promoting a healthy lifestyle is reduced dietary salt intake.

SALT AND BLOOD PRESSURE

Scientific evidence that links dietary salt intake with an increase in blood pressure is irrefutable. Current dietary recommendations for salt intake are five grams per day, which is about a tip of a teaspoon, but research has shown that in most countries, salt intake is double or triple this value. The major sources of dietary salt besides that which is added during food preparation include fast food, canned foods, bread, and processed meats like bacon. The mechanism suggested for the relationship between increased dietary salt intake and hypertension is that salt increases the concentration of body fluids, resulting in stimulation of thirst and increased water intake. This causes an increase in total body water, including plasma, which is part of blood. Consequently, blood pressure increases because of increased fluid volume in the arteries.

FRUITS AND VEGETABLES REDUCE HIGH BLOOD PRESSURE

Current focus on the management of hypertension is on antihypertensive drugs. Even though there is a push to manage hypertension with medication, high blood pressure is still poorly controlled in most parts of world. As a result, there has been increased interest in the role of one's diet in the control of blood pressure. There is a lot of scientific evidence that shows the relationship between longevity and vegetarian diet. In a study published in America, called "Dietary Approaches to Stop Hypertension" (DASH), people were divided into three groups and given three different diets. The first group was given four daily servings of fruits and vegetables, the second group was given eight servings of fruits and vegetables, and the third group was provided with ten servings of fruit and vegetables. There was a significant reduction in blood pressure in the two groups taking eight and ten servings of vegetables. Even though all fruits and vegetables are important in the management of hypertension, because of their high potassium content, some fruits and vegetables have received interest because of their special antihypertensive properties. The fruits and vegetables listed below contain special antihypertensive properties.

Garlic

Garlic has become a focal point for clinical research because of its blood-pressure-lowering properties. Findings from the studies have shown that garlic can be an effective complementary therapy for hypertensive patients. There is mounting scientific evidence that demonstrates the antihypertensive properties of garlic. These include:

- Generation of hydrogen sulphide
- Reduction of the synthesis of vasoconstrictors
- Increase in the concentration of nitric oxide
- Inhibition of angiotensin-converting enzyme

The biochemical mechanisms listed above are very similar to those found in antihypertensive medication. This highlights the importance of garlic in the management of hypertension. The production of hydrogen sulphide is one of the mechanisms responsible for the antihypertensive effects of garlic. Our red blood cells use the polysulphides in garlic to produce hydrogen sulphide, which vasodilates (expands our blood vessels), resulting in the reduction of blood pressure. Garlic also reduces blood pressure by inhibiting formation of an enzyme called "angiotensin II." This enzyme increases blood pressure in two ways. First, it constricts blood vessels, which causes an increase in blood pressure. Secondly it stimulates the release of a hormone called "aldosterone." This hormone causes the kidneys to reduce salt excretion, thus increasing the amount of salt in the body. An increase in salt leads to increased blood pressure. By blocking the activity of angiotensin II, garlic causes a reduction in blood pressure. Though garlic is effective in reducing blood pressure, it cannot be used as a replacement of antihypertensive medication; it can only be used as a supplement. Hypertensive people should continue taking their blood pressure medication during the Daniel Fast.

Besides its antihypertensive properties, garlic has been found to have many cardiovascular protective properties (ability to protect the heart and blood vessels). This is due to its ability to reduce inflammation, cholesterol, triglycerides, and formation of oxygen radicals. Inflammation and oxidative stress damage the inner lining of blood vessels leading to a number of cardiovascular problems like strokes, heart attacks, and atherosclerosis (deposition of fat and calcium in the walls of the arteries). Two compounds in garlic are known to produce its anti-inflammatory properties. These are "1,2-vinyldithiin" (1,2-DT), which inhibits an inflammatory factor called "NF-κB", and "thiacremonone," which reduces secretion of interleukin 6 (IL-6) and interleukin 8 (IL-8) by macrophages. Garlic is also rich in two important nutrients, selenium and manganese, which are cofactors with important antioxidant reactions. Selenium is a cofactor of an enzyme called "glutathione peroxidase," which is a powerful antioxidant. Manganese is a cofactor of another enzyme called "superoxide dismutase," which also plays an important role in the destruction of oxygen radicals.

Garlic also contains a compound that protects our blood vessels from becoming blocked. It contains a disulphide which has been shown to have anticlotting properties. It prevents platelet (cells in the blood responsible for formation of blood clots) aggregation, which is a crucial step in blood clot formation. For platelets to form a blood clot, they become sticky and clump together. The disulphide compound in garlic prevents the platelets from becoming sticky, thus inhibiting formation of a blood clot. Garlic gives a unique flavor to food, and should form part of the daily diet in hypertensive people. To get the full nutritional benefits of garlic, it has to be eaten raw. For those who cannot eat raw garlic, they can add it to the food toward the end of the cooking process.

Strawberries

Strawberries are very important in the regulation of blood pressure. Besides their high content of potassium, which has been shown to reduce blood pressure, they also upregulate endothelial nitric oxide synthase (eNOS). This enzyme catalyzes the production of nitric oxide (a compound that causes vasodilation) from L-arginine. Notric oxide lowers blood pressure by:

- Inhibiting entry of calcium into cells
- Activating potassium channels, leading to hyperpolarization
- Stimulating dephosphorylation of myosin light chains

The three mechanisms above lead to vascular smooth muscle relaxation. As the smooth muscles of the blood vessels relax, blood pressure is reduced.

Brown Rice

Brown rice is a rich source of magnesium, which, as previously discussed, has been shown to play a significant role in the regulation of blood pressure. Magnesium is a natural antagonist of calcium in the body. Calcium is a very important mineral that plays an important role in bone metabolism and many other cellular activities (including muscle contraction and nerve cell function). Its other important role is the prevention of excessive blood loss by mediating blood clot formation. When levels of magnesium are low, calcium can have a negative effect by increasing cardiac and smooth muscle tone resulting in increased blood pressure. In people who consume magnesium-rich diets like brown rice, the activities of calcium are well-regulated. Besides regulating calcium, magnesium has been shown to reduce the blood pressure by increasing the body's levels of nitric oxide.

As stated earlier, hypertension is the major risk factor for cardiovascular diseases, which are the leading killers in the world. The Daniel Fast is one of the important tools in the fight against hypertension, as there is mounting evidence that shows that fruits and vegetables have special properties that lower blood pressure.

Chapter 11

The Daniel Fast for Teenagers

"TRAIN A CHILD IN the way he should go, and when he is old he will not turn from it" (Prov 22:6). It is important for parents to train their teenage children about the importance of drawing close to God with prayer and fasting. The diet for teenagers who partake in the Daniel Fast must be closely monitored and safely regulated, because they are going through a very important phase of life. Their nutritional requirements are influenced by the events of puberty and the growth spurt. Their height and weight is increasingly due to the rapid growth of body organs. This accelerated growth rate requires specific nutrients that may be deficient in a plant-based Daniel Fast diet. It is for this reason that the diet of teenagers needs special consideration.

NUTRITIONAL REQUIREMENTS FOR TEENAGERS

Proteins

Proteins are needed for maintenance of the accelerated growth rate of the body's organs. Protein deficiency could result in adverse conditions in teenagers, since the accelerated growth rate is dependent on protein metabolism. The Daniel Fast excludes animal products like meat, eggs, and dairy, which are rich in protein, because it is a calorie-restriction diet. This makes it unsuitable for adolescents. However teenagers are part of the Christian family, so therefore they must partake in the Daniel Fast. This dilemma can be solved by creating a Daniel Fast diet that is suitable for teenagers. The special diet will be discussed later in this chapter. Below is a list of nutrients that are essential to teenagers.

Minerals

The accelerated rate of growth in teenagers requires three important minerals: calcium, iron, and zinc.

Calcium

The body's requirements for calcium in adolescents are greater than they are in either childhood or adulthood because of increased skeletal growth during the teenage years. Almost 99 percent of the body's total calcium is found in the skeleton. For normal skeletal growth, teenagers require food that is rich in calcium. A low calcium intake during adolescence could result in low bone density, which may predispose teenagers to frequent fractures or osteoporosis later in life.

Iron

Iron is required for the synthesis of red blood cells to provide adequate oxygen for growing body organs and increasing muscle mass. In girls, intake must be sufficient to balance the iron lost in menstruation. Deficiency of iron could lead to muscle weakness and constant fatigue due to anemia.

Zinc

Zinc is very essential for sexual maturation in adolescents. It is associated with a number of proteins that are required for protein formation and gene expression. Deficiency results in growth retardation and hypogonadism. Teenagers must follow a diet that is rich in zinc for normal sexual development.

Vitamins

Teenagers require food that is rich in vitamins for normal growth. The development of the reproductive and immune system requires vitamin A. Vitamin D is essential for the mineralization of bones to ensure that they are strong.. The increased growth rate requires adequate supply of vitamin C, which is essential for collagen synthesis. During adolescence, cell growth is increased—therefore, the vitamin "folate" is required, because it plays an important role in DNA synthesis.

PARTIAL DANIEL FAST FOR TEENAGERS

For reasons explained above, the health of teenagers may be compromised if they enter into the full Daniel Fast. Abstaining from food for long periods (from midnight to 6 p.m. in the evening) may affect growth. Therefore, it is advisable for teenagers to enter into a partial Daniel Fast. A partial Daniel Fast meal plan is as follows:

- Breakfast: Whole grain cereal; e.g., oats or sorghum (mabele) with soy milk. If cereals are not preferred, then one slice of whole wheat bread may be taken instead. Sugar-free and caffeine-free tea can be taken. Plant-based mono- or polyunsaturated margarine may be added to the bread or cereal.
- Lunch: One fruit.
- Supper: A full meal of fruits and vegetables.

FRUIT AND VEGETABLE DIETS SUITABLE FOR TEENAGERS

All the dietary requirements listed in the previous sections make the Daniel Fast difficult for teenagers, because it excludes animal products like meat and dairy. Animal products are rich in proteins, minerals and vitamins required by teenagers. A strict fruit and vegetable diet may be deficient in calcium, zinc, iron, vitamin D, and vitamin B12. For the Daniel Fast to be suitable for teenagers, it must be modified to meet their dietary requirements. Teenagers who embark on a strict fruit and vegetable diet are at risk of suffering from nutritional deficiencies. On the other hand, if a diet is carefully planned, it can meet all the dietary requirements of teenagers. In the next section I will suggested foods that are suitable for teenagers. Parents may modify the diet as they wish, but I strongly advise against giving teenagers a nutrient-deficient diet during the fast.

VEGETABLE SOURCES OF IRON

During the twenty-one-day Daniel Fast, iron-rich meat and its products are not consumed. This could be detrimental to teenagers who require a lot of iron. It is therefore very important that during this period they eat iron-rich vegetables. The challenge is that vegetable-based iron is not easily absorbed. This is not a crisis, because a certain combination of fruits and vegetables promotes iron absorption; for example, foods rich in vitamin C. Eating a serving of iron-rich vegetables with lemons or oranges promotes iron absorption. Tea and coffee should be avoided during this period, because they contain "tannins" which prevent iron absorption.

Sorghum

Sorghum is a relatively cheap source of iron compared to meat. It also contains copper, which helps the uptake and absorption of iron. This promotes red blood cell synthesis, preventing conditions like anemia. Increased red blood cell synthesis is very crucial to the rapidly developing teenage body, because it increases oxygen delivery to the tissues, promoting cellular growth and repair.

Green Leafy Vegetables

Green leafy vegetables are considered as rich sources of non-heme iron. A serving of spinach, about one hundred grams, contains 20 percent of the recommended daily allowance of iron. Even though the iron in spinach is not easily absorbed because it is non-heme, spinach is also rich in vitamin C, which promotes iron absorption.

Legumes

Legumes like beans, peas, and lentils are very rich in iron. One cup of lentils contains 37 percent of the recommended daily allowance of iron. Since the iron in beans is not easily absorbed, beans must be consumed in combination with vitamin C-rich foods like tomatoes, citrus fruits, and green leafy vegetables.

NON-MEAT SOURCES OF PROTEIN

While animal products like meat are good sources of protein, there are a number of plant-based protein sources that are suitable for the Daniel Fast.

- Lentils: A delicious source of protein. Not only do they have protein, they also have fiber that regulates bowel function.
- Kidney beans: One of the richest sources of non-meat protein. When combined with whole grains, such as brown rice, they provide high-quality protein that is compatible with that of meat. In addition to providing protein, they are a good source of cholesterol-lowering fiber, and they stabilize blood sugar.
- Soy milk: Rich in proteins, and can make a good substitute for cow milk. Some studies have shown that it helps in the prevention of cancer.

- Green peas: A delicious source of protein that contains the amino acid "leucine," which is rare in plant-based foods.
- Peanuts: A good source of protein that is rich in monounsaturated fats. This makes peanuts good for heart health.
- Oats: Have three times more protein than brown rice. It is also a good source of calcium which is necessary for skeletal growth in teenagers.

VITAMIN B12 SUPPLEMENTS

Vitamin B12 is only found in animal-based products, and the Daniel Fast excludes animal-based products—therefore, teenagers partaking in the Daniel Fast could become vitamin B12-deficient. To avoid this, people partaking in the Daniel Fast (especially teenagers and the elderly) must take vitamin B12 supplements. Vitamin B12 is one of the most essential nutrients required for rapidly growing teenagers. It is required for the synthesis of DNA and RNA, which are the body's genetic material. Both these compounds, known as "nucleic acids," are necessary for cell division. Vitamin B12 is also essential in the synthesis of red blood cells and the health of nerve cells—therefore, deficiency of vitamin B12 in young people can result in serious symptoms like fatigue, diarrhea, nervousness, shortness of breath, numbness, and/or tingling sensations in the fingers and toes. It is crucial for teenagers to take vitamin B12 supplements during the fast. These supplements come in different forms, such as capsules, tablets, lozenges, and gels. They can also be administered through the nose as intranasal sprays. It is advisable to consult a health care professional before taking these supplements to avoid complications or interactions with other medication.

Parents have a God-given responsibility to teach their children spiritual disciplines, like fasting. Most importantly, it must not be enforced on the children. They have to be taught about the saving grace of God, so that when they fast, they don't just do it to please their parents, but they do it in humble submission to their heavenly Father.

Chapter 12

The Daniel Fast for the Elderly

IN THE BIBLE, OLD age is seen as a blessing. In the book of Psalms, for example, it is bestowed upon those who love God: "Because he holds fast to me in love, I will deliver him; I will protect him, because he knows my name. When he calls on me, I will answer him; I will be with him in trouble; I will rescue him and honor him. With long life I will satisfy him and show him my salvation" (Ps 91:14–16). It is also seen as a blessing to those who are righteous:

> "The righteous shall flourish like a palm tree and grow like the cedar of Lebanon. They are planted in the house of the LORD; they flourish in the in the courts of our God. They still bear fruit in old age; they are forever fresh and green, declaring that the LORD is upright, he is my rock and there is no unrighteousness in him" (Ps 92:12–15).

From these verses, it is clear that God blesses his children with longevity. Sadly, this blessing does not manifest in the lives of many Christians because of unhealthy eating habits. Unless there is a drastic change in the lifestyle habits of Christians and a healthy diet becomes a compulsory part of a Christian lifestyle, the blessing of longevity will remain elusive to many. Pastors have to adopt this healthy lifestyle and preach it on their pulpits. There are many studies that have linked longevity to diet. In previous chapters we have discussed how a fruit-and-vegetable-rich diet prolongs life by reducing incidence of cancer, diabetes, and hypertension. Most of these conditions, like heart failure and cancer, are linked to age-related deaths. Since all of those positive dietary changes are important for the elderly, it is important for them to partake in the Daniel Fast.

THE AGE PARADOX

If someone were to ask how old you are, I am sure you would give them your chronological age (the number of years you have lived). We typically determine our age from the chronological number of years we have been alive; however, this is not our only age. We also have a biological age, which is the age of the organs and systems in our bodies. It is determined by the length of the telomeres in our chromosomes. The shorter the telomeres, the older we are biologically and the longer the telomeres, the younger we are. Biological age and chronological age run parallel, but not at the same speed. An incongruity may exist between them. This discrepancy exists because biological age is not just a forward mathematical progression of time, like numerical age, but it can stand still, accelerate, or reverse. This means that, biologically, the aging of our organs can remain still, accelerate, or they may be renewed. At any given point in time, biological age may not be the same as our chronological age. Based on this differential, organs can be older or younger than an individual's numerical age.

Chronological age is beyond our control. It always flows forward depending on speed and gravitational force. According to Einstein's theory of relativity, as the gravitational force or speed increases, time slows down. On the other hand, we can control our biological age, as it is determined by our genes and lifestyle choices. Good lifestyle choices, like exercise and eating a healthy diet, reduce the biological age, and our organs become younger than our chronological age. Bad lifestyle choices like smoking, drinking alcohol, overeating, and eating fatty foods will have an opposite effect of making our organs older than our chronological age. That is why the Daniel Fast is important for the elderly. It can be a period of organ regeneration and renewal. For reasons that will be explained below, the fasting program cannot be as rigorous as that of younger people.

VITAMIN B12 DEFICIENCY

Again, since vitamin B12 is only found in animal-based products, elderly people face a risk of vitamin B12 deficiency if they partake in the Daniel Fast. This is serious for the elderly, because vitamin B12 deficiency is implicated in age-related visual impairment, due to macular degeneration. Macular degeneration can eventually lead to blindness. Supplementation with vitamin B12 reduces the risk of the development of macular degeneration. Though vitamin B12 supplementation is recommended, it can interact with other medications that are taken by the elderly, like Colchicine, which is used to treat gout, and Metformin, which is used to control blood sugar levels in diabetic patients. This means that animal products should not be completely eliminated from the Daniel Fast diet of the elderly.

PROTEIN DEFICIENCY

Dietary protein intake is more important in the elderly compared to younger individuals. Age-induced muscle mass loss is associated with increased body fat. To preserve muscle mass, old people require sufficient dietary protein intake. Studies have shown that elderly patients who do not consume enough animal protein lose both bone and muscle mass. Since the Daniel Fast prohibits animal product consumption, the elderly could suffer serious protein deficiencies.

REDUCED GROWTH HORMONE SECRETION

In chapter 4, we indicated that meat consumption is detrimental to health, due to increased levels of IGF-1. In the elderly, the situation is completely different. Reduced meat consumption is associated with increased mortality. The reason is reduced growth hormone secretion in the elderly. This decline in growth hormone results in reduced IGF-1, which may result in impairment of bone formation and increased risk for fractures.

CALCIUM DEFICIENCY AND BONE MASS REDUCTION

The elderly are at a very high risk of bone fracture because of age-induced bone mass reduction, and women are at a higher risk compared to men. Women lose about 42 percent of their spinal bone mass with age. The most common cause of bone resorption (reduced bone mass), is calcium deficiency in the diet. Furthermore, the elderly cannot produce pro-vitamin D in response to ultraviolet light as younger people. This leads to reduced gastrointestinal calcium absorption. Older people can be adversely affected by the Daniel Fast, because animal products are the richest source of vitamin D. It is important for the elderly who wish to partake in the Daniel Fast to take calcium and vitamin D supplements under the supervision of a health care professional. Studies have shown that elderly people who receive calcium and vitamin D supplements have reduced osteoporotic fractures.

DIETARY SALT INTAKE

Research has shown that age is the strongest predictor of high blood pressure. The most common type of hypertension in the elderly is isolated systolic hypertension. In this condition, systolic blood pressure is abnormally increased, while diastolic blood pressure remains unchanged. This causes an increase in pulse pressure (the difference between systolic and diastolic blood pressure). The increase in pulse pressure is caused by increased arterial stiffness due to aging. Increased pulse pressure is dangerous, as it is associated with target organ damage; for example, it is one factor that damages aging kidneys. As a result, kidney function is reduced in the elderly. Since dietary salt is excreted through the kidneys, impaired function will result in reduced salt filtration in the kidneys. Consequently, more salt will be retained by the kidneys, causing an increase in salt in the body. The high salt content will cause an increase in blood pressure. The age-related changes reduce the kidney's ability to excrete salt, therefore dietary salt reduction should form part of the Daniel Fast eating plan in the elderly. Due to these age-related changes such as reduced kidney function, reduction in dietary salt intake is essential for the control of blood pressure in the elderly.

THE EYES

Besides the effects of Vitamin B12 deficiency discussed earlier in relation to eye problems, reduced antioxidant vitamin intake has also been linked to eye problems. People with high vegetable intake do not suffer from eye-related problems like macular degeneration. The most common eye problem in the elderly is development of cataracts, and this has been shown to occur less in elderly people who eat adequate amounts of fruits and vegetables. A daily serving of fruits and vegetables reduces the oxidative damage of the eye lens.

PROSTATE PROBLEM

One of the leading risk factors for prostate cancer is age. The risk for prostate cancer is in males who are fifty years old and above. This risk increases with age. This cancer develops in the prostate glands of males. It can spread from the prostate to other parts of the body. It is a very slow-growing cancer, so the person can have it for years without showing any symptoms. It is for this reason that men who are forty years and above should go for annual prostate checks. The most common symptom of prostate cancer is difficult urination. Symptoms that develop later, when the disease has progressed, include blood in the urine and pelvic pain when urinating.

Risk factors for prostate cancer include age, obesity, a fatty diet, reduced sexual activity, and genetic factors. Though there is no evidence from any studies, we can speculate that the Daniel Fast can provide some level of protection from prostate cancer. A diet rich in fruits and vegetables has many cancer-fighting properties. The other benefit could be weight reduction, due to the low caloric state of the Daniel Fast diet.

PARTIAL DANIEL FAST FOR THE ELDERLY

Like teenagers, the elderly should enter the Daniel Fast with caution. Any form of dietary restriction could be detrimental to the elderly. A partial Daniel Fast is recommended for people who are sixty-five and above. They should continue eating animal products like meat and dairy, but abstain from processed meat like bacon. Sugar, sugary drinks, fast foods, canned foods, and processed carbohydrates should also be avoided.

Conclusion

A DIFFERENT TYPE OF revival is needed in the church worldwide, a revival that will integrate spiritual rebirth with physical regeneration. Spiritual revival that does not incorporate physical health gives birth to a church that is heavenly minded but useless on earth. As ambassadors on this earth, we need healthy bodies to fulfill our God given mandate. The fact that Jesus' ministry incorporated both spiritual and physical healing is a clear indication that Jesus cared for our physical bodies as much as he cared for our spirit. In the book of John, he states that "I have come so that they may have life and have it in abundance" (John 10:10). It is not possible to have life in abundance with a sick body. To experience abundant life, Christians have to take care of their bodies, as they are the temple of the Holy Spirit.

"My people are dying because of lack of knowledge" (Hos 4:6). The meaning of this verse is clearer today than ever before. Christians view drunkenness and drug addiction as sin, but when it comes to food addiction they are very liberal. All of these addictions, whether alcohol, drugs, or food, lead to death; but Christians have conveniently accepted food addiction as normal. If a study could be conducted in the church to determine which of these three addictions kills more Christians, probably gluttony will take the number one spot. Lack of understanding of the Scriptures has made gluttony acceptable in the church. In the book of Proverbs, gluttony is contrasted with obeying God's law: "He who keeps the law is a discerning son, but a companion of gluttons disgraces his father" (Prov 28:7).

Why is gluttony so prevalent in the church? In spite of all the dietary advices and fads that Christians follow, the incidence of obesity is high in the church. The reason could be that obesity is not just a physical problem, but a spiritual condition. The most common reason for overeating is that people feel good when they eat. There is a rewarding feeling that accompanies eating. It serves as an escape mechanism. The person may be trying to escape from a spiritual void that keeps on coming back when they finish eating. By overeating, they are trying to close the spiritual void with food. They do not eat because they are hungry physically, but spiritually. Overeating is not the main problem, but a symptom of a deeper spiritual problem. That is why a spiritual solution like the Daniel Fast is a perfect intervention method for obesity. As we fast, we solve the physical problem by eating fruits and vegetables that heal our bodies, resulting in the reduction of obesity. The most important outcome, though, is that the root cause of the physical problem, which is spiritual, is also solved. Therefore, if the Daniel Fast program outlined in this book is followed diligently, for those twenty-one days we will walk with God like Enoch, and when we finish the fast, we will reflect God's glory like Moses.